D0349079

DRYING FLOWERS

A step-by-step guide to creating,
decorating and preserving.

Pamela Westland

DRYING FLOWERS

A step-by-step guide to creating, decorating and preserving.

Pamela Westland

NEW BURLINGTON BOOKS

A QUINTET BOOK

Published by New Burlington Books
6 Blundell Street
London N7 9BH

Copyright © 1991 Quintet Publishing
Limited. All rights reserved. No part
of this publication may be reproduced,
stored in a retrieval system or
transmitted in any form or by any
means, electronic, mechanical,
photocopying, recording or otherwise,
without the permission of the copyright
holder.

ISBN 1-85348-334-6

Reprinted 1992, 1995

This book was designed and produced
by Quintet Publishing Limited
6 Blundell Street
London N7 9BH

Creative Director: Terry Jeavons
Designer: Stuart Walden
Project Editor: Judith Simons
Editor: Karin Fancett
Photographer: Ian Howes

Typeset in Great Britain by
Central Southern Typesetters, Eastbourne
Manufactured in Hong Kong by
Regent Publishing Services Limited
Printed in Singapore by Star Standard Industries Pte. Ltd.

CREDITS
All photography © Ian Howes/Quintet
Publishing Ltd, with the exception of pages 48/49;
© Paul Forrester/Quarto Publishing plc.

Contents

Introduction

I F YOU HAVE EVER WALKED AROUND A beautiful and well-stocked garden in summer and wished you could capture the ambience for ever – you can. Drying flowers and preserving foliage are ways of suspending nature, of holding plant materials at the peak of their condition and in all their glorious array of colour.

Until you have time to build up a selection of materials you have preserved for yourself, specialist shops offer an ever-increasing variety of dried flowers and seedheads, a tapestry of different textures, shapes and sizes that enable you to start designing with flowers straight away.

However, no shop-bought materials can give you quite the same satisfaction as those you have chosen to preserve for yourself, and no shop can offer the range that you can gradually build up by cutting a few stems from a garden here and a hedgerow there. Add those to the exotic materials you can buy, and the repertoire of materials at your fingertips will be enormous.

Drying flowers and foliage is a simple matter, and at its simplest just involves hanging them in a warm, airy place. Some materials need more than air drying, and later we explain the processes of drying flowers in desiccants, and preserving foliage and bracts in a glycerine solution.

Once you have accumulated a collection of long-lasting materials, you will want to use them in designs all around your home. We tell you how to make sure that these designs are at one with their surroundings, and how to choose the container, the colour

BELOW
A delightful summer garden, closely planted with flowers and plants of every colour, shape and texture, will provide a rich harvest of materials for drying and preserving

scheme and the style of arrangements so that they will fit perfectly in your home.

Dried flowers are infinitely versatile, and the ways of arranging them are many and varied. In one chapter we tell you how to create exquisite posies for a bride to carry and enchanting posies to enhance your home. We explain how to make floral swags and ribbons to decorate a room for always or a church for special occasions, and how to create floral circlets and rings as permanent indoor displays and as festive decorations.

Throughout the book, we show you in simple step-by-step photographs how to create designs you will be proud of, and which will delight your friends. In short, we show you in the easiest possible way how to decorate with dried flowers.

CHAPTER ONE
Drying and Preserving Plant Materials

T HE WONDERFUL THING ABOUT THE ART of drying flowers is that you do not need any special equipment, nor do you even need to buy the plant material. We are all surrounded in our everyday lives by plant material that is eminently suitable for drying and will give long-lasting pleasure after any one of several simple drying processes.

If you have a garden then, as we shall see, the scope is immense, from border flowers and herbs to vegetables and even twigs. If you have access to a friend's or neighbour's garden then you might be allowed to rescue some seedheads that would otherwise – what a waste! – have been consigned to the rubbish heap; lupins, for example, which look like silvery-grey velvet pods, and mallow which are like silver stars.

If you have bought an impulse bunch of flowers you might decide to dry one or two of them and slowly build up a dried collection – daffodils dried in desiccant, or a stem of mimosa dried in a container, perhaps. And if you have been given a florists' bouquet or spray of flowers you might decide, for sentimental reasons, to dry some of the flowers as a lasting memento.

If you have the chance to go for a walk in the country, in a wood or even on waste ground you might find a treasure trove of items to dry – cones, acorns, nuts, rampant weeds and their seedheads, grasses, wild oats by the wayside, gnarled twigs and pieces of wood in interesting shapes. Remember that it is against the law to pick wild flowers in a wide range of categories; if you are in any doubt, play safe and do not pick any.

LEFT
The delicate trumpet-shaped flowerheads of springtime daffodils can be dried in desiccant and used to decorate the home throughout the year.

BELOW
Several herbs, such as sage with its bright blue or mauve flowers, can be dried successfully, adding another dimension to these useful culinary plants.

GROWING PLANTS
FOR DRYING

One of the greatest joys of owning a garden is harvesting flowers, seedheads and other plant materials for drying. There is a special thrill in going from plant to plant, a basket over your arm, gathering flowers which, after a simple drying process, you can enjoy in arrangements for months to come.

You may like to gather flowers from here and there in the borders and beds, a stem or two of midnight-blue delphinium captured at the peak of perfection, a few rosebuds, a bunch of pink and white clarkia, a handful of poppy or rue seedheads, whatever you have. Or, if you are already a dried-flower enthusiast, you may perhaps have a small area, like a kitchen garden, set aside to grow flowers specially for drying.

It is a good idea to do this, for a number of reasons. For one thing, having a dried flower patch enables you to grow flowers in rows, maximizing the use of the space and facilitating harvest. It is much easier to keep an eye on a row of flowers, gathering a few each day as they reach prime condition, than it is if they are scattered around the garden among other plants. Not only that, you can grow flowers for drying regardless of their size and scale in relation to your borders and beds, and regardless of their overall visual appeal. No plant is too tall and unwieldy, nor too small and insignificant to grow in a 'working patch', whereas it might look out of place in a mixed border.

If you do consider planting a dried flower patch, this is the place to grow all the everlastings, the flowers that dry to a papery crispness on the plant and form the foundation of many a dried flower collection. These include strawflowers in shades from palest peach to deepest crimson; winged everlasting with its yellow-domed, white daisy-like flowers; sunray (swan river) everlasting in deep pink and purest white; and statice in all its artist's-palette range of colours. Try to find space, too, for the

ABOVE
Delphiniums and the smaller larkspur are handsome border plants, much used in dried-flower decorations. They should be harvested for drying when the topmost flowers are still in bud.

yellow-flowered silver-leaved (white-leaf) everlasting, for feverfew with its tiny white domes of flowers, for love-in-a-mist which dries at both the baby-blue flowering stage and the seedhead stage, and for the delicate bush-like plants of gypsophila, sometimes called baby's breath, in both white and pink. On a larger scale you might like to include a plant or two of golden rod, a large subject with small-scale design potential, tansy with its generous clusters of tiny golden flowers, and achillea (yarrow) in

TOP & ABOVE
Achillea (yarrow) with its flat-topped clusters of yellow, pink, or cream flowers, and fluffy spires of golden rod are large-scale plants which adapt well to the drying process.

varieties which provide you with flat-topped clusters of yellow, cream, pink and white flowers, all excellent candidates for drying.

Some plants are worth growing, either in a working patch or in a border, for their decorative seedheads. These include poppy, honesty, teasel and rue, which all have definite design appeal when mixed with other dried materials.

Make room, too, either in your working patch or a corner of the garden, for ornamental grasses, which make such a

ABOVE
Tiny white yellow-centre feverfew (Chrysanthemum parthenium) will provide a delicate touch to dried-flower designs.

RIGHT
*Decorative seedheads,
such as teasels, provide
neutral tones, bold shapes
and strong textures to a
design.*

pretty neutral foil to more showy and colourful dried materials. You can buy packets of mixed ornamental grass seed which include quaking grass, hare's-tail grass and many others that have an attractive part to play in floral designs.

Do not overlook the vegetable garden in your quest for suitable materials for drying. Onion and garlic seedheads, chive and marjoram flowers, corn-on-the-cob (corn) heads, sorrel seeds and globe artichokes – as varied a group of plant materials as it would be possible to imagine – all dry well and extend the range of your collection.

If your dried-flower garden is confined to a small patio, a balcony or even just a couple of windowboxes, there is still scope for variety. You might have tubs of mop-headed or lace-cap hydrangeas, which dry well by air drying; lady's mantle with its fluffy clusters of lime-green flowers; miniature roses, one of the most charming of dried materials; and pink and blue cornflowers which retain their brilliant colours perfectly. All the everlastings can be planted in pots, tubs and troughs, and are good value; they have an extended flowering period, providing colour and interest long before they are ready for harvesting.

HARVESTING

Just as it is with cereal and other food crops, so it is with flowers and other materials for drying. If they are to dry satisfactorily, retain their form and colour, and give pleasure for many months to come, they must be harvested when conditions are just right and they are in peak condition.

Naturally the weather plays a key role; it can be very frustrating to see flowers just becoming ready to cut when torrential rain arrives. It is important to gather flowers and seedheads when they are absolutely dry and carrying no excess moisture. This means harvesting them on a dry day and at certain times of the day, once the early morning dew has dried off and before the evening

LEFT
The vegetable garden can be a rich source of materials for drying. Chives, with their pink, dome-shaped flowerheads, are a member of the onion family and dry well.

BELOW
Flowers and foliage should be harvested in peak condition.

DRYING AND PRESERVING PLANT MATERIALS

Lavender is an easy and decorative plant to grow in casual clumps, or in pots and troughs. Lavender spires retain their heady scent when dried and are ideal for use in aromatic dried-flower designs for the bedroom; or simply crush the flowers and add to a pot-pourri blend.

dew settles. When harvesting flowers (it does not matter about seedheads) it is advisable to avoid midday, when the sun is at its highest, since the flowers tend to wilt rather than begin the drying process slowly and surely. This means, then, that the ideal time for your floral harvest is mid-morning and mid- to late afternoon.

Capturing the various types of flowers at the right stage for drying calls for a fine degree of judgement. Those for air drying need to be cut before they are fully opened. In the case of long spike-like flowers, such as delphinium, the smaller larkspur and clarkia, this means gathering them when a few of the flowers at the base of the stem are fully opened, those higher up are partly opened and the topmost ones are still in bud. Roses are a special case: you can cut them in tight bud, when they will dry readily, retaining their closed, tightly-furled form, or when the buds have started to unfurl but before they are fully open.

If you plan to dry flowers in a desiccant (see below) you can harvest them at a later stage, just as they become fully open. Leave them a day or two later, though, and you might find the results disappointing.

Examine each stem or flower before you start and discard any blemished or damaged materials. It may be possible, in the case of roses for example, to pluck off one or two discoloured outer petals, leaving the remainder of the flower in perfect condition, or in the case of seedheads to pull off a few damaged specimens at the base of the stem. Do not be tempted to waste time and space by drying imperfect materials. Damaged petals are likely to rot and could then affect other materials around them.

Strip off all lower leaves from flower stems, especially those that would be trapped by the string when tying them in bunches. Crunched up and without a free circulation of air, the leaves would rot and affect the rest of the plant material.

AIR DRYING

Air drying is the simplest and the most widely used method of drying plant material. All you need is space in a dry, warm room with a free circulation of air. The temperature should not fall below 10°C/50°F and there should be no induced moisture in the air. This rules out a steamy kitchen, utility room or bathroom. An airing cupboard, the space over or around a central heating boiler, a spare bedroom, an attic or loft or, in summertime, a shed or garage may all be suitable. Bear in mind that plant materials can look highly decorative throughout the drying process and you might add the sitting room or dining room to the list of possibilities.

Plant materials can be air dried by one of several methods. Plants can be hung individually or in bunches, stood upright in a roomy container, laid flat on shelves or racks, placed in boxes or wound around a horizontal pole. Some plants will dry successfully by only one method and others offer a choice. In the latter case, the size and type of drying area you have available may then be the deciding factor on which method you choose.

Whatever the method, it is important that air can circulate around the materials as they dry, since air is the only drying medium employed. This means making up small bunches with the flowerheads staggered and separated from each other, hanging some large stems such as delphinium and hydrangea individually, or choosing a wide-necked container so that stems can fan out away from each other, allowing plenty of space all around them as they dry.

To dry materials by hanging, gather the stems into bunches, just a few specimens in each, and tie them with raffia or twine. Hang the bunches upside-down on wire coat-hangers, on strings or rods suspended across a room corner, on coat-hooks (as long as the materials hang away from the wall surface) or on clothes airing racks.

All the everlasting flowers, including strawflowers, winged everlasting and statice, may be dried in this way. Other candidates include materials made up of a mass of tiny flowers or florets which, as they dry, shrivel almost imperceptibly and retain their original form. Among the flowers in this category are hydrangea, golden rod, tansy, achillea (yarrow), mimosa, lady's mantle, larkspur and clarkia; and the seedheads include poppy, love-in-a-mist, mallow, lupin and rue. Chinese lanterns, most brilliant of all seedheads, are stripped of all their leaves and dried by hanging, and

ABOVE
A cool collection of materials air-dried by hanging. There is quaking grass, hare's-tail grass, silver-leaved (white-leaf) everlasting and lady's mantle.

so are rosebuds, stripped of only their lower leaves. Rose leaves closer to the flower head furl attractively as they dry and become a feature of the dried plant material.

Very few leaves can be dried successfully by air drying, though sage is an exception. Both green and purple sage leaves furl most attractively in the hang-drying process and are a useful addition to a collection.

WIRING STEMS BEFORE DRYING

Some flowers may need to have false wire stems attached before they are dried. These include strawflowers which frequently snap from their brittle stems and multi-flora roses which grow in clusters on short stems.

- *To wire strawflowers, push a medium-gauge stub wire up through the base of the flower and out through the top. Bend over a small hook, like a hairpin, and pull it down into the flower centre where it will be concealed.*

- *To wire roses, place a stub wire against the short stem and bind the two together, using silver roll wire or fuse wire. Take the binding wire down beyond the stem, twisting it until it is secure.*

- *Hang the wired flowers in bunches to dry, easing out the wire stems so that the flower heads are not touching each other.*

- *Once the flowers are dried, the false stems can be covered with gutta-percha binding tape to conceal them (see page 35).*

Plant materials which can be dried upright in a dry container include sea lavender, feverfew, bulrushes, corn-on-the cob (corn) heads, globe artichokes, onion seedheads and pampas grass. Other plants – although it sounds a contradiction in terms – may be dried by standing in water. These include hydrangea, mimosa, gypsophila, cornflower and pearl everlasting. Pour about 5cm/2in of

ABOVE
Some of the stateliest of dried materials – bulrushes, pampas grass and hogweed – are dried upright in a container.

water into a wide-necked container such as a casserole dish or large preserving jar and stand the stems so that the ends are under water. As the stems gradually absorb the water it evaporates and the plant material naturally dries.

Some plant materials dry most successfully when placed flat on absorbent paper – for example – on racks or shelves. All grasses give good results in this way. Dock and sorrel seedheads, giant hogweed and lavender, are others that do well. Place the materials in a single layer on the paper and turn them carefully every day or so, so

LEFT
*Linseed, sea lavender
and a selection of grasses
can also be dried by
standing upright, well
spread out, in a container.*

that each part of the plant material is uppermost in turn.

Mushrooms and other fungi can be dried by hanging (thread a piece of string through them and hang the string across the airing cupboard) or by being placed on absorbent paper. Make sure that the fungus is perfectly dry before you start the further dehydration process. If it is the slightest bit moist it will simply rot. Check caps and stems for insects, too. It is worth noting that the warm air that is needed for drying provides just the right nursery conditions favoured by all kinds of creeping creatures.

Pine and fir cones, a harvest you can gather during a walk in the woods, dry well by being placed on a shelf or in a box in a dry, warm room. Try to gather a collection of different sizes and shapes so that you have enough for designs of all kinds. Horse chestnuts, or conkers (buckeyes), another treasure from the countryside, dry well in boxes and make glossy highlights, especially in winter arrangements.

Climbing plants, such as clematis, old-man's-beard and hops, dry most attractively if you wind them around a pole suspended horizontally, perhaps across a room corner.

ABOVE
*Immersing the stems in a
small amount of water is
one way to dry hydrangea
heads and gypsophila.*

Once dry, these twisty-twirly stems are most effective if they are used to outline an arch, above a door architrave or along a window pelmet.

The time taken to air-dry flowers and other plant materials will vary considerably according to the moisture content of the materials and the temperature and humidity of the room. In a warm airing cupboard a stem of delphinium could be dry in two or three days. In a cooler shed or garage it could take eight to ten days to reach the stage when it is safe from developing mould. Test your materials every two or three days. Flowers and leaves are ready when they sound and feel as crisp as tissue paper, and seedheads when they feel very light and crisp.

DESICCANT DRYING

If air drying is considered to be the completely natural way to dry flowers, seedheads and other materials, then drying in a desiccant, or a drying agent, may be thought of as the more scientific means. Instead of relying on a free circulation of air, this method employs dry granules or powder to draw out the moisture from the flower petals. It is suitable for a wide range of flower types and, as we have said, may be used to preserve fully opened flowers.

The principle is to cover every part of the surface area of every petal with the drying agent, which then draws out the moisture evenly and completely. The story goes that the method was first discovered several centuries ago by a cook on a large English estate. She is said to have buried rose petals in powdered sugar to scent it, ready to make delicate confections. When she came to remove the petals, she found that they had retained their colour, form and shape perfectly and were, quite simply, dried versions of their former selves. And so a new technique was born!

In fact, powdered sugar is not now recommended as a drying agent, as it has a tendency to become sticky as it absorbs moisture. The most popular and effective desiccant is silica gel crystals which you can buy in some chemist shops (drug stores). They are available in standard white or in a colour-indicated form, blue crystals which turn pink as they absorb moisture and become damp. You need to grind them down to at least half of their original size, using a pestle and mortar or a blender.

Other suitable drying agents are borax and alum powders, both available from some chemists (drug stores), and dry silver sand. The powders may be used alone but they tend to cling to the dried petals, leaving a white film which is difficult to brush off. It is best to use three parts powder mixed with two parts silver sand. The sand may be used alone for large plant materials such as mop-head chrysanthemums and dahlias, but never for small flowers, since its weight would crush them.

To dry flowers in this way, sprinkle a thin layer of the desiccant, about 1cm/½in, in the base of a biscuit (cookie) tin that has a tight-fitting lid. Place the flowers on the drying agent, spaced well apart and not touching each other, sprinkle on more desiccant so that it fills any hollows in the flowers – the trumpets of daffodils for example – and brush it lightly to cover all the petals. A small camel-hair brush is most suitable for this delicate task. When all the flowers are covered, sprinkle on a thin layer of the desiccant, put on the lid and set the tin aside where it need not be moved.

If you use silica gel crystals check the flowers after two to three days and remove them as soon as they are dry. Leaving them in the crystals for too long makes them impracticably brittle. If you use a chemical and sand mixture, check the flowers after about six days. Carefully remove the lid, taking care not to shake up the contents of the tin. Brush aside the top layer and check one flower for dryness.

When the flowers are dry, carefully remove them from the desiccant – tweezers are useful for this – and brush away any clinging powder or crystals with the camel-hair brush.

1 *A shallow layer of ground silica gel crystals forms a base for cosmos and nasturtium, the first stage in the desiccant drying process.*

2 *The crystals are sprinkled over the flowers to cover them, and then the box is covered with the airtight lid. The flowers should be dry in two to three days.*

The purchase of any of these desiccants can be a once-in-a-while event since they can be used over and over again. After using the drying agent sieve it to remove any plant particles that may have become detached, spread it on baking trays and dry it in a low-temperature oven, when the colour-indicated silica gel crystals will return to blue. Allow the desiccant to cool, then store it in an airtight tin or jar.

The desiccant drying method is suitable for preserving composite flowers such as daisy, marguerite, spray chrysanthemum, gerbera (Transvaal daisy) and marigold; 'hollow' flowers such as daffodil, narcissus, lily, orchid and freesia; flat-faced flowers such as buttercup, camellia, anemone and pansy; and a host of others. You can dry separate flowers from a stem of delphinium; complete stems of lily-of-the-valley and grape hyacinth; tightly clustered flowers such as ranunculus and zinnia; or fully opened roses and peonies – the list is endless, and is limited only by the amount of desiccant, space, time and plant material you have available.

To prepare flowers for desiccant drying you need to cut off all or most of the stem, and, while the flower is still supple, insert or wire on a short length of stub wire, the foundation for a false stem to be bound on once the flower has been dried. See page 14 for the method.

Once they are dried, flowers can be stored between tissues in a box or drawer. And once they have been bound on to a full-length wire stem they can be stored upright, the stems inserted in a piece of dry foam and angled so that the flowers do not touch or crush each other.

MICROWAVE DRYING

Air drying and desiccant drying are traditional methods of preserving flowers which have been practised for generations. Now a new method has come on the scene, drying in a microwave oven. This is a technique to experiment with, taking snippings of flowers and foliage and testing to see how well they preserve. In general terms, the method is suitable for small sprays of many of the plant materials that can be preserved by air drying, but is not suitable for composite or 'hollow' flowers, which just collapse.

The exact time taken to dry will depend on the moisture content of the plant material and on the volume being processed, but on average most flowers and foliage sprays are dried after approximately three to four minutes on full power.

Place a piece of kitchen paper in the centre of the microwave – or on the turntable, if you have one – and arrange flowers and foliage sprays well apart, so that they are not touching. Check them after three minutes on full power and give them extra time if they are not fully dehydrated.

Among flowers that dry well in the microwave are marjoram and lady's mantle, both composed of a multitude of minute flowers; cornflowers, composed of a mass of tiny petals; silver-leaved (white-leaf)

ABOVE
Cream, pink, red and blue cornflowers dried in a microwave retain all the depth and subtlety of their colours.

everlasting, tansy, double white feverfew, and *Chrysanthemum parthenium* 'Golden Ball'. Pansy flowers are something of a hit-and-miss affair, giving passable results most times. If they emerge looking slightly crumpled, they can be coaxed back to their pristine shape by being pressed under a heavy weight for an hour or so.

Most leaves shrivel unrecognizably under the heat of this method, but among the successes, also in three to four minutes on full power, are fennel, sage and many of the silver-leaved evergreen plants.

PRESSING

Pressing flowers and leaves, a hobby that takes many of us back to our childhood, is another way of drying and preserving plant material, one that leaves the subjects somewhat brittle, and one-dimensional. Pressed flowers do not have much of a part to play in three-dimensional dried flower designs, but leaves can be useful. One advantage that pressing leaves has over preserving them in glycerine is that they can be captured at any time of year, not just when the sap is rising in the plant.

Effectively, this means that you can press fallen autumn leaves in all their glorious colours, from russet to gold, from scarlet to yellow, and use them to complement dried flowers in arrangements. The pressed leaves can be mounted on false wire stems and angled this way and that in designs, to give contrasting textural interest, visual weight at the base, and brilliant natural colour.

To press leaves you can use a standard flower press or you can use the traditional method of pressing leaves between sheets of absorbent paper in a heavy book. You can even press large leaves between sheets of newspaper placed under the carpet in a busy-thoroughfare area of a room. Once dried, the leaves can be stored between tissues in a box, or kept in a book.

It is a simple matter to mount pressed leaves on wire. According to the size and type of leaf, you can thread a stub wire in and out of the leaf along the central vein, or stick a wire along the centre of the leaf, using narrow florist's tape.

SKELETONIZING

Skeletonized leaves, in which all the plant tissue has been eroded away, make delicate and attractive additions to a dried collection. You can sometimes find them beneath a magnolia or holly bush, a lacy shadow of their former selves, leaving just the vein structure of the leaf. Other leaves, besides magnolia and holly, that are suitable for skeletonizing include ivy and laurel.

To prepare skeletonized leaves by the traditional method involves leaving them in a pot of rainwater for weeks on end, a slimy process that will eventually break down the plant tissue and enable you to brush it away from the veins. A quicker and cleaner method is to boil the leaves in a cup of blue household detergent powder in a pan of water for about 30 minutes. Wash the leaves under a cold tap and then, using an old toothbrush, brush away the broken-down tissue. Wash the skeletonized leaves again and, if you wish, immerse them in water with a little household bleach to freshen the colour. Blot the leaves between sheets of blotting paper until they are completely dry, and store them between tissues in a box.

ABOVE
Ethereal skeletonized holly leaves can be wired together for use in a dried flower decoration.

PRESERVING IN GLYCERINE

Preserving foliage, bracts and berries in a glycerine solution greatly extends the range of long-lasting plant materials, offering you a collection of supple, glossy leaves which harmonize perfectly with the matt texture of dried flowers. All leaves change colour during the process, many of them taking on the deep russety-brown tints of autumn and a warm, copper-kettle kind of homely glow – just the look for arrangements you can enjoy throughout the winter.

Beech, one of the most popular leaves to preserve, turns a deep chestnut brown; laurel turns such a dark brown that it is almost black; eucalyptus emerges from the process in a new deep gunmetal blue guise; and rosemary and bay turn deeper shades of green. Rose hips and berries shrink a little and some fade slightly. Red berries mellow to a deep orange, yellow berries (of holly, for example) turn deep golden orange, and blackberry fruits retain all the glorious depth of their colour.

The principle of the technique is simple, and one that cheats nature to a decorative advantage. The preserving solution is made up of one part glycerine to two parts very hot water. This is taken up by the stems and carried to every part of the plant material. As the water evaporates the glycerine is retained by the plant cells and preserves the material in its entirety. According to the size and type of the plant material, the process can take from a few days to several weeks.

The process is suitable for all deciduous and evergreen leaves, and for bracts such as bells-of-Ireland. The material must be gathered after the leaves are mature and while the sap is still rising in the plant, and so this places it as a summer pastime. You can store and re-use any left-over solution again, topping it up each time with the correct ratio of glycerine and water.

Inspect all foliage stems carefully and snip off any damaged or discoloured leaves or bracts. Strip off lower leaves and any that would be damaged by being trapped in the container. Scrape off the bark from woody stems for about 5cm/2in from the base, and split or gently crush the stem ends so that they can more readily take up the solution.

Make up the solution, pour it into a lidded jar and shake it vigorously until it is thoroughly mixed. Pour it into containers (any type will do) to a depth of about 5cm/2in and stand the stems in it, making sure that their ends are submerged.

ABOVE
Pyracantha berries and rose hips, fern leaves and bells-of-Ireland bracts can all be preserved in a glycerine and water solution.

Some large, fleshy leaves are best preserved by being totally immersed in the solution. These include aspidistra (cast-iron plant), fig and *Fatsia japonica* (Japanese fatsia). Pour the solution into a shallow dish and immerse separate leaves.

Check the material every few days. Top up the containers with more of the solution if it has all been absorbed before preservation is complete. If the tips of the leaves start to dry out – and this can happen with some large specimens – rub them on both sides with cotton wool soaked in the solution. If beads of moisture appear on the surface, this is a sign that the plant material is already saturated with the solution, and should be removed straight away. The material is ready when the leaves or bracts have evenly changed colour and are completely supple. There should be no sign or sound of brittleness.

Once it is ready, remove the material from the solution. Dry stems thoroughly and wipe large leaves with cotton wool or a soft cloth to remove any stickiness. Dry immersed leaves thoroughly and 'polish' them with a dry cloth. Store preserved leaves flat in boxes or upright in containers in a cool, dark room. The stems can safely be used in arrangements with both fresh and dried flowers, and will not absorb any further moisture.

ABOVE
Once preserved, long stems of escallonia with their minute leaves can be used to make effective outlines in a design.

TOP
Berberis (barberry) leaves will turn dark brown during the preserving process.

TIME CHART FOR PRESERVING FOLIAGE IN GLYCERINE

The following table will give you some ideas of leaves to preserve, and the approximate time taken for the process.

MATERIAL	NOTES	APPROXIMATE NUMBER OF WEEKS TO PRESERVE
Aspidistra (cast-iron plant)	Immerse in solution	2–3
Bay	Leaves deepen to dark green	2
Beech	Cut when fully mature. Preserve in large or small sprays	½–1
Bells-of-Ireland	Hang upside-down to dry after preserving	3
Berberis (barberry)	Preserve long stems. Leaves turn dark brown	3
Blackberry	Treat sprays of leaves complete with berries	3
Cotoneaster	Leaves turn leathery brown, silver on reverse	3–4
Cypress	Treat flat fan-shaped leaves complete with 'cones'	3–4
Dock	Treat long spikes of seedheads, which turn a deeper shade of red	2
Escallonia	Treat long stems of the minute leaves. They make good outlines in designs	2
Eucalyptus	Leaves darken and retain their gunmetal appearance	2–3
Fatsia japonica (Japanese fatsia)	Immerse in solution. Leaves turn leathery brown	2–3
Fig	Immerse single leaves	1–2
Hellebore	Leaves turn light brown	3
Holly	Treat sprays of leaves and berries. Spray berries with hair lacquer	3
Ivy	Immerse very large leaves. Treat stems complete with berries	1½–2 3

TIME CHART FOR PRESERVING FOLIAGE IN GLYCERINE		
Laurel	Leaves turn almost black	4
Mahonia	Leaves sometimes give two-tone effect	3–5
Maidenhair fern	Can preserve leaves at any time of year	2
Maple	Treat single leaves and clusters of keys	2
Mistletoe	Treat small sprays with berries	2
Oak	Oak-apples and acorns can be preserved on the stems	2–3
Old-man's-beard	Gather before flowers open. Spray with hair lacquer after preserving	2
Peony	Leaves turn dark olive green with light contrasting veins	2
Pyracantha	Treat sprays with berries	3
Raspberry	Leaves turn dark red with silver undersides	2
Rhododendron	Preserve leaf sprays with young, tight buds	3
Rose	Young shoots of wild roses preserve well. Boil solution to preserve	2
Rose hips	Spray hips with hair lacquer after preserving	2–3
Rosemary	Leaves retain their scent	2
Rowan (mountain ash)	Preserve sprays of leaves and berries. Leaves turn nut brown	2–3
Silver birch	Use solution at boiling point	4
Sweet (Spanish) chestnut	Preserve some with catkins	1½–2
Sycamore	Treat leaves and keys	1–1½
Viburnum	Leaves turn deep brown with olive green on reverse	3
Yew	Leaves can be preserved at any time. Berries are not reliable in the preserving process; they often wither	3

ABOVE
Sprays of holly – together with their berries – can be preserved in glycerine. Red berries take on a rich orange hue.

ABOVE
Preserve sprays of rhododendron when the flowers are in bud.

BELOW
Viburnum leaves will turn dark brown with olive green on the reverse when preserved in glycerine.

ABOVE
*Large fleshy leaves such
as fig and ivy can be
preserved flat, completely
immersed in the glycerine
and water solution.*

METHOD CHART FOR DRYING PLANT MATERIALS

The following table provides a guide to just some of the plant materials you can dry by the methods described earlier in this chapter. It is, of course, by no means a complete list of all the possibilities, which are endless.

MATERIAL	PART OF PLANT MATERIAL TO BE DRIED	METHOD
Acanthus	flower	air drying
Achillea (yarrow)	flower	air drying
Anemone	flower	desiccant
Astilbe (spirea)	flower	air drying
Bell heather	flower	air drying
Bells-of-Ireland	bracts	air drying and glycerine
Broom	short flower sprays	desiccant
Bulrush	seedhead	air drying
Buttercup	flower	desiccant
Camellia	flower	desiccant
Campion	flower	air drying
Carnation	flower	desiccant
Celosia cockscomb	flower	air drying
Chamomile	flower	air drying
Chinese lantern	seedhead	air drying
Chive	flower	air drying
Chrysanthemum	flower	desiccant
Clarkia	flower	air drying
Clematis	leaves and seedheads	air drying
Copper beech	leaves	air drying and glycerine
Cornflower	flower	air drying and microwave

ABOVE
Fluffy spires of astilbe (spirea) are most effectively dried by air drying.

25

BELOW
Delicate cornflowers are suited to air or microwave drying.

ABOVE
*Dahlia flowerheads
should be dried in
desiccant and then stored
in a box between tissue
paper to preserve their
shape.*

BELOW
*'Air dry' hydrangea
bracts by standing them in
a wide-necked container
holding approximately
5 cm/2 in of water.*

METHOD CHART FOR DRYING PLANT MATERIALS		
Corn-on-the-cob (corn)	seedhead	air drying
Daffodil	flower	desiccant
Dahlia	flower	desiccant
Daisy	flower	desiccant
Delphinium	flower	air drying and desiccant
Dock	seedhead	air drying
Dryandra	flower	air drying
Eryngium (sea holly)	flower	air drying
Fennel	leaves	microwave
Fescue grass	seedhead	air drying
Feverfew	flower	air drying and microwave
Forsythia	short flower sprays	desiccant
Giant hogweed	seedhead	air drying
Globe amaranth	flower	air drying
Globe artichoke	seedhead	air drying
Golden rod	flower	air drying
Grape hyacinth	flower seedhead	desiccant air drying
Gypsophila	flower	air drying
Holly	leaves	skeletonizing
Honesty	seedhead	air drying
Hop	leaves and flowers	air drying
Hydrangea	bracts	air drying
Ivy	leaves	skeletonizing
Jerusalem sage	flower, leaves and seedhead	air drying

METHOD CHART FOR DRYING PLANT MATERIALS

Laburnum	short flower sprays	desiccant
Lady's mantle	flower	air drying and microwave
Larkspur	flower	air drying and desiccant
Laurel	leaves	skeletonizing
Lavender	flower	air drying
Lilac	small flower sprays	desiccant
Lily	flower	desiccant
Lily-of-the-valley	flower	desiccant
London pride	flower	desiccant
Love-in-a-mist	flower and seedhead	air drying
Love-lies-bleeding	seedhead	air drying
Lupin	seedhead	air drying
Magnolia	flower leaves	desiccant skeletonizing
Mallow	seedhead	air drying
Marjoram	flower	air drying and microwave
Millet	seedhead	air drying
Mimosa	flower	air drying
Narcissus	flower	desiccant
Old-man's-beard	leaves and seedhead	air drying
Onion	seedhead	air drying
Pampas grass	seedhead	air drying
Pansy	flower	desiccant and microwave
Peony	flower	air drying and desiccant
Pine	cone	air drying
Pink	flower	air drying

TOP & ABOVE
*Small sprays of lilac and
lily flowers can be
successfully dried in
desiccant.*

BELOW
*Once the flowers have
died back, poppy
seedheads can be air dried.*

DRYING AND PRESERVING PLANT MATERIALS

ABOVE
Senecio leaves, air- or microwave-dried, will add subtle colour and texture to a design.

BELOW AND BOTTOM
Sweet peas and wallflowers should be dried in desiccant to preserve their delicate shapes.

METHOD CHART FOR DRYING PLANT MATERIALS

Polyanthus	flower	desiccant
Poppy	seedhead	air drying
Pot marigold	flower	air drying and desiccant
Quaking grass	seedhead	air drying
Ranunculus	flower	desiccant
Rose	bud, flower and leaves fully opened flower	air drying desiccant
Rue	seedhead	air drying
Sage	flower leaves	air drying air drying and microwave
Sea lavender	flower	air drying
Sedge	seedhead	air drying
Senecio	leaves	air drying and microwave
Silver-leaved (white-leaf) everlasting	flower	air drying
Sorrel	seedhead	air drying
Statice	flower	air drying
Stock	flower	desiccant
Strawflower	flower	air drying
Sunray (swan river) everlasting	flower	air drying
Sweet pea	flower	desiccant
Tansy	flower	air drying and microwave
Timothy grass	seedhead	air drying
Wallflower	flower	desiccant
Winged everlasting	flower	air drying
Zinnia	flower	desiccant

CHAPTER TWO

Tools and Techniques

A BUNCH OF GYPSOPHILA IN A WINE JUG making a natural 'lace curtain' in a cottage window; a blue and white jug of statice in a sunny breakfast corner; a silver vase of dainty pink rosebuds on a dressing table – it is possible to compose pretty arrangements of dried flowers with no special equipment at all. However, by using a selection of stem-holding materials, wires and tapes – equipment which is known as mechanics – it is possible to greatly extend the range of containers you can use and thus the designs you can achieve. It would, for example, be very difficult to arrange a glorious basket of peonies, lavender, marjoram and globe thistle for a summer fireplace with no hidden support for the stems. Dried flower stems are brittle and wayward, and when massed together have a habit of thrusting upwards and outwards if they are not tamed in some way.

STEM-HOLDING MATERIALS

New enthusiasts to the art of decorating with dried flowers may shy away from using stem-holding materials, thinking that they add a complication and make natural-looking designs more difficult to achieve. In fact, the reverse is true. By using some kind of support for the stems, the element of chance is eliminated, and the arranger can concentrate more fully on the design he or she wishes to create.

The principal stem-holding material, made specially for use with dried flowers, is dry foam; this is available in a block a little larger than a household brick, in small cylinders, and in spheres, cones and rings of various sizes. The foam may be brown or grey, is as light as a feather and has a slightly sparkly surface. It must be emphasized that its fresh-flower counterpart, absorbent foam (which is usually green), should not be used in its unsoaked state for dried flower arrangements, since it does not give the necessary degree of grip and is, besides, liable to break up.

The dry foam blocks may be used in their entirety for large designs; indeed two or more bricks may be needed for arrangements on large pedestals or in wide baskets. You can also think of the blocks as a designer-friendly raw material you can cut to any size and shape, to fit or fill any type of container and help you to achieve any design you have in mind. All you need is a sharp knife to cut the foam and a sheet of newspaper to cover your working surface and catch the shiny dust that comes away when the foam is cut.

The cylinders, about 5.5cm/2¼in deep and 8cm/3in across, may be used alone, wedged into the neck of a container such as a teapot or coffee pot, for example, or used in conjunction with plastic saucers specially made for the purpose, with a ridged indentation that exactly matches the diameter of the foam.

The spheres may be used to create designs such as a dried flower hanging ball. A pretty

GLISTENING GLASS

YOU WILL NEED:

GLASS CONTAINER

FOAM–HOLDING PLASTIC

SAUCER

ADHESIVE CLAY

SMALL CYLINDER OF DRY FOAM

–

HONESTY

SEA HOLLY

APRICOT STATICE

WHITE SEA LAVENDER

APRICOT STRAWFLOWERS

BLUE LARKSPUR

1 *The glass vase is fitted with a white plastic saucer, held in place with a ring of adhesive clay. The small cylinder of dry foam exactly fits into an indent in the saucer.*

2 *Short stems of honesty, echoing the pattern on the vase, are positioned to form a triangular shape.*

3 *The spiky outlines of the sea holly contrast effectively with the smooth discs of honesty.*

4 *Apricot statice introduces a warm colour to the design. The foreground is filled with white sea lavender.*

5 *The round, full faces of the apricot strawflowers stand out against the contrasting shapes which form the basis of the design. The blue larkspur follows the outlines and intensifies the colour value.*

example would be a ball composed of delicate grasses and, for a countryside look, deep blue cornflowers to hang in a window or an alcove. Foam spheres are also used to create indoor trees, the small and medium sizes for table-top designs and the large size for a floor-standing model.

The cones are used for pyramid designs and may be used alone, when the foam shape is placed on a dish or board, or to create a stylized 'topiary' tree, when the shape is mounted on a twig or cane and set realistically in a flower pot or other container (see page 78).

Dry foam rings are used to create wall or table-top designs, circlets of dried flowers and seedheads to grace any room from the bedroom to the kitchen. Designs of this kind are described fully in Chapter Four.

The other principal stem-holding material is 5cm/2in-wide wire-mesh netting which you can buy by the metre or the yard from garden-supply shops, where it is also known as chicken wire. Florists and some floral art clubs sell a more refined version in which the netting is coated with green plastic. To use the netting you crush it into a mound or ball and wedge it to fill the neck of a container. This may be an urn, a wide-necked vase, a deep bowl or a basket. As the wire is scrunched up it forms an entangled mass with uneven but smaller-than-original holes – just what is needed to anchor and angle dried flower stems.

Florists' setting clay, sold packaged in lumps of various weights, can be used as a stem holder, although that is not its main purpose. The green clay may be used on, for example, a woven placemat if you want to create a flower spray on the textured background. A small lump of the clay pressed on to the surface will hold the stems firmly – and permanently, since it soon sets as hard as cement.

Another use for setting clay is to anchor the 'trunk' element of designer table-top trees into their pots. Larger trees are usually set in plaster of Paris, a cheaper material more suited to the quantity needed for floor-standing designs.

Pinholders may be used with dried as well as fresh flowers. These heavy weights with vertical spikes are available in various shapes and are especially useful for designs built up on a flat surface such as a board or tray. Stems can be pressed between the spikes to stand upright or to angle this way and that. Large preserved or pressed leaves can be included in the base of the design to conceal the holder, or it may be masked by a handful of gravel or marble chippings.

FIXING MATERIALS

Adhesive clay (not to be confused with setting clay) is an extra-tacky clay which is used to secure, for example, a plastic foam-holding saucer to the neck of a container. You may decide to turn a glass wine carafe into a pedestal by fitting it with a saucer of foam. A few dabs of adhesive clay around the rim secures the saucer in place.

The clay is also used to fix plastic spikes to a container. These four-pronged spikes can be used to hold foam in place. First press a dab or two of the clay on to the base of the spike. Press it in place in the container and then press on the foam. The clay is sold in strips, on a reel or in cut lengths. It is dark green, about 1cm/½in wide and sold with a paper backing. The surfaces it is used on must be completely dry, but once it is in place it will not be dislodged by subsequent moisture.

Florists' adhesive tape, which is sticky on one side and sticks well to non-porous and shiny surfaces, is useful to fix foam firmly into containers. Used from side to side, up and over the foam and down on to the container, it does a belt-and-braces job of reinforcing any other means of securing the foam. It is not usually necessary to take this extra precaution with small designs but it is a worthwhile insurance when large containers are used. The tape can also be used in addition to adhesive clay to fix plastic foam-holders to other containers.

YOU WILL NEED:

TALL VASE

CHICKEN WIRE

FLORISTS' ADHESIVE TAPE

—

PRESERVED AND DRIED

BELLS-OF-IRELAND

LINSEED SEEDHEADS

GREEN WHEAT

ACHILLEA (YARROW)

FEVERFEW

1 *The container, a green and yellow 1940s jug, is fitted with a mound of crumpled chicken wire held in place with two criss-crossing strips of florists' adhesive tape.*

2 *Tall stems of bells-of-Ireland bracts, some dried and some preserved in glycerine solution, match the subdued colours of the jug.*

3 *In complete contrast to the stately stems already in place, the ball-like linseed seedheads form a wayward shape and extend the width of the design.*

4 *Green wheat, keeping well within the colour framework, is positioned in clusters.*

5 *The flat heads of achillea (yarrow) and the bunches of yellowing feverfew give weight between the narrow and upright stems.*

POSY BASKET

YOU WILL NEED:
FLAT SHALLOW BASKET
PLASTIC PRONG
ADHESIVE CLAY
PIECE OF DRY FOAM
BLUE PAPER RIBBON
STUB WIRE
—
GOLDEN WHEAT
YELLOW ROSEBUDS
BLUE LARKSPUR
BLUE BROOM BLOOM
WHITE FEVERFEW
YELLOW ACHILLEA (YARROW)

1 *A plastic prong is secured to the base of the basket with a dab of adhesive clay. Then the small piece of foam, cut from a large block, is impaled on the spikes.*

2 *First to be arranged in this illusionary posy design are the heads of golden wheat, their stems cut in short and graduated lengths.*

3 *Yellow rosebuds are positioned between the wheat, some with their stems cut so short that the flowers nestle against the holding foam.*

4 *Blue larkspur, adding an intensity of colour, is arranged to fill in the spaces. Again, many of the stems are cut to very short lengths.*

5

6

5 *Now the illusion grows. The posy stalks, all cut from wheat, are positioned in the other side of the foam to make a fan shape. Some extend just beyond the rim.*

6 *The posy is built up: blue broom bloom and white feverfew both complement the colour scheme and provide a contrast of shape.*

7 *A few short stems of yellow achillea (yarrow) are inserted between the rosebuds and then the bow is added, a flourish of paper ribbon mounted on a bent stub wire.*

7

WIRING

Many of these mechanics will be familiar to anyone used to designing with fresh flowers, since the method of preparing the containers is similar. One technique which applies more specifically to dried flower designs is wiring: wiring flower heads on to false stems; wiring short natural stems on to longer wire ones; extending natural hollow stems by inserting a wire; wiring bunches of small-scale materials together to make a massed effect (for example, snippings of golden rod) and wiring dried cones, nuts and other materials to decorate swags and ribbons. In short, the technique of wiring has an important part to play in dried flower design, and is one that should be practised until it can be achieved quickly, easily and above all neatly.

We saw in Chapter One that some flowers, strawflowers especially, are apt to part company with their natural stems and need to be given false ones, in this case a medium-gauge stub wire. Stub wires are available in several thicknesses, from fine through medium to heavy gauge, and in lengths from 9 to 45.5cm/3½ to 18in. Usually two or three types of stub wire will be sufficient; there is certainly no need to invest in the whole range!

Fine silver binding wire, very similar to fuse wire, is used to bind stub wires to short lengths of natural stem when, for example, flowers have been dried in desiccants. This wire is sold in rolls and is sometimes known as rose wire. A good tip when using it is to place the roll in a cup so that it does not roll off the table or get tangled. A heavier-gauge reel wire, which may be black or brown, is useful when wiring dried materials to swags and rings.

Lengths of split cane, sold in bundles by some florists, are used to provide or lengthen stems of heavy-headed flowers such as chrysanthemums and pom-pom dahlias – any flowers, in fact, which would be top-heavy if they were mounted on a

wire. If such flowers have no natural stem at all, it will be necessary to mount them on a heavy-gauge stub wire, pushing it up from the base of the flower, bending over a short hook and pulling that through into the flower centre. The length of wire extending beneath the flower can then be bound on to a cane, using fine roll wire.

Cones have many decorative uses in dried flower designs, and are especially appreciated in winter arrangements and those made for Christmas. To wire cones and give them a false stem use a heavy or medium-gauge stub wire, according to the size of cone. Wrap one end of the wire inside and around the lowest row of scales leaving 5cm/2in of the wire jutting out. Twist the two ends together tightly and bend them to form a straight stem beneath the cone. If the cone is to be inserted into a foam shape such as a ring, this stem length should be sufficient. If it is to be used in an arrangement it will be necessary to wire on a full-length false stem. Place a split cane or heavy-gauge stub wire against the short stem and bind the two together with silver roll wire.

ADDITIONAL EQUIPMENT

- *Gutta-percha tape – available in light and dark green, cream, and brown – for binding and concealing wire stems.*

- *Wire cutters for trimming wire mesh and thick stub wires.*

- *Florist's scissors for cutting flower stems and lighter-gauge wires.*

- *Secateurs (pruning shears) for cutting woody stems and branches.*

- *Clear fast-drying glue to attach dried materials to containers for a decorative effect; or nuts and cones to swags or rings; and to stick blocks of foam together.*

A Handful Of Stems

YOU WILL NEED:
GLASS FISH-BOWL VASE
—
BUNCH OF DRIED HOGWEED STEMS
LAVENDER
BLUE LARKSPUR
RED ROSEBUDS
RED MINIATURE ROSES
PRESERVED AND BLEACHED EUCALYPTUS LEAVES

1 *The dried hogweed stems, cut to equal lengths, are arranged in a glass fish-bowl vase to form a tightly packed twist.*

2 *First to be positioned in the cluster of hogweed stems are short lengths of lavender, arranged in bunches of six or seven stems.*

3 *Blue larkspur, cut to match the lavender in length, reinforces the colour and strengthens the mass of near-vertical lines.*

4 *Red rosebuds and clusters of miniature roses begin to soften the geometric lines of the design and add a bright colour element.*

5

5 *Pale cream, translucent eucalyptus leaves bring a third, and contrasting shape to the design. The natural twist and twirl of the leaves is particularly striking against the erect hogweed stems.*

COUNTRY BASKET

YOU WILL NEED:
BASKET
BLOCK OF DRY FOAM
MEDIUM-GAUGE STUB WIRES
—
WHEAT
BLUE LARKSPUR
PINK RHODANTHE
PINK STRAWFLOWERS
WHITE SEA LAVENDER

1 *A whole block of dry florists' foam fits neatly from side to side of this basket, and needs no fixing.*

2 *A fan shape of wheat, the stems of roughly equal length, forms the basis of the arrangement.*

3 *Matching the wheat almost stem for stem, short lengths of blue larkspur begin to fill in the spaces.*

4 *Clusters of sugar-pink rhodanthe are wired into small posies. Each medium-gauge stub wire extends below the flower stems and is used as a false stalk.*

5 *As the deeper pink strawflowers are added, the colour and shape contrast builds up.*

6 *Spiky stems of white sea lavender make a perfect filling material. Here they are used to good effect throughout the design, spilling over the container rim at the front.*

5

6

Making pot-pourri is an extension of the art of drying flowers, and adds another dimension to decorating the home. A bowl of tactile, colourful pot-pourri is a delightful and natural way to scent a room.

Traditionally, pot-pourri is made of scented flowers such as roses, lavender, pinks, sweet pea, jasmine, honeysuckle, hyacinth, freesia and orange blossom, and aromatic leaves such as bay, rosemary, lemon thyme, lemon balm, rose geranium, marjoram and peppermint.

Your kitchen spice rack will yield many of the popular spices that give pot-pourri the depth of its aroma. These include cardamom, coriander, cinnamon, allspice, mace, nutmeg, cloves and star anise.

To hold the scents of the dried plant materials and spices you need a fixative such as dried orris root powder which is available from herbalists and some chemists (drug stores), and to intensify the aroma you need a few drops of an essential plant oil, such as rose, lemon or neroli.

Pot-pourri should be as personal as a scent. Adapt the following recipe to suit your own preferences.

8 CUPS SCENTED PETALS AND FLOWERS
2 CUPS LAVENDER FLOWERS
1 CUP AROMATIC LEAVES
15ML/1TBSP GROUND CINNAMON
5ML/1TSP GROUND CLOVES
60ML/4TBSP GROUND ORRIS ROOT POWDER
3–4 DROPS NEROLI OR OTHER ESSENTIAL PLANT OIL

● Spread the flowers, petals and leaves on baking trays and dry them in an airing cupboard for several days, or in the oven at a low temperature. When dry, they should be crisp, and feel and sound papery.

● Tip them into a jar, add the spices and orris root and stir well. Cover the jar and leave it for 8–10 weeks, shaking or stirring it frequently.

● Add the oil and cover the jar. Leave for another 7 days.

● Finally, transfer the pot-pourri to decorative bowls, or put it in sachets and bags to scent clothes cupboards and drawers.

● Alternatively, pot-pourri can be used as part of a dried-flower design to disguise stem-holding materials in a glass container (see page 42).

PREPARING CONTAINERS

The degree of care taken in preparing containers pays dividends in the finished design. And again, with a little practice, it is a technique which can be quickly and easily mastered.

When some kind of holding material is needed, as it is with shallow, wide-necked or large containers, the first question is whether to use dry foam or crumpled wire-mesh netting. In general, foam is preferred for shallow containers such as bowls and dishes and chicken wire for deep ones such as fish-bowl-shaped vases and most baskets. But there are exceptions, and in many cases the two materials are interchangeable.

To shape foam to fit the base of a shallow bowl, press the bowl on to a block of foam to make an indent, then cut around it. If the bowl is a wide one, it may be necessary to stick or tape two blocks together. Using a sharp knife, sculpt the foam to come to a dome shape in the centre, with an even, gentle curve sloping down at the sides. Press a plastic spike in place in the base of the container with adhesive clay and push the foam firmly on to the prongs.

If you want to angle some stems horizontally in the design, or have them slanting downwards over the rim of the container, shape the foam to extend about 5cm/2in above the rim. This extra height will then enable you to position stems at any angle you wish.

Glass containers pose a special problem, because dried flower stems and taped artificial ones do not look well when massed in the base of a container. If you are using a tall glass vase or wine carafe you can turn it into a simulated pedestal by fitting a foam-holding saucer and a cylinder of dry foam to the top in the way described earlier. The stems will all be held high above the container, and the holding material concealed behind flowers and leaves pressed close against the foam. Designs of this kind often puzzle people who are not in the know, who wonder why no stems are visible within the container.

If you use a wide-necked glass trough, you can tackle the situation in a completely different way by concealing a block of foam inside it. Cut the foam to almost fill the rectangular container, but leaving a cavity on all four sides. Firmly fix the foam in place on a plastic prong, then fill the gap between the dry foam and the glass walls with a decorative natural material. This could be pot-pourri, in a mixture chosen to colour-blend with the dried flowers in the arrangement (see page 40). It could be dry sphagnum moss which has an interesting texture and gives a casual country look. Or it could be lichen moss which has silvery highlights and is especially attractive if you pick up this element by using the silvery filaments of honesty 'moons' in the design.

There is nothing difficult about using crumpled wire in the neck of a container. Take a piece of wire in both hands, tuck in the exposed ends and crush it into a ball to fit the neck of a container. If you are using a valuable container or one which will scratch, tape all round inside the rim with adhesive tape to protect the surface. Secure the wire to the container in whatever way is appropriate. You can wire it to the handles of a basket, using stub wires or roll wire, or fix it to a ceramic container by criss-crossing adhesive tape over the wire netting and down on to the container. Test the wire for movement and add more fixing if it is still mobile. For most designs it is best to shape the wire into a dome which curves gently into a mound above the rim of the container. This will enable you to position some stems at a rakish angle whereas, if the wire were flat, the stems could only be positioned vertically.

Obviously, whenever you use a stem-holding material of any kind it is important to conceal it completely. The slightest glint of the silvery finish on dry foam blocks not only gives the game away, but spoils the look of the design. Recessing flowers and leaves into the heart of the design, and having some materials on very short stems is one way of ensuring concealment. Another way – leaving you more flexibility in the design – is to cover the foam with a layer of sphagnum moss anchored in place with bent stub wires used as staples. If traces of the natural moss are visible in the finished design all is not lost. Furthermore, the material adds textural interest and an extra dimension to the arrangement.

Moss can be used in other decorative ways, too. You can convert the most utilitarian household container – anything from a plastic ice-cream tub to a shoe box – by covering it with a thick layer of dry sphagnum moss, hay, or a mixture including some dried flowers. Paint the surface of the container with clear, quick-setting glue and press on handfuls of moss or hay. If you have a few dried marjoram flowers, for example, to add colour to the covering, so much the better. Add more and more of the mixture until the surface is completely covered then, partly for a practical purpose, partly for decoration, tie the container around with two or three bands of plaited raffia. Containers converted in this way look lovely with a country-style mass of dried decorative seedheads.

If you have an open-weave basket or one that needs a face-lift you can decorate it with dried stems of lavender or thyme, weaving or sticking them all over the basket, around the rim or over the handle. Lavender baskets made in this way are expensive to buy, and especially attractive when arranged with dried flowers.

The natural colour of baskets and woven plant materials is particularly complementary to dried flowers. But there may be times when you feel that a design would benefit from a closer colour link between the container and its contents. Painted baskets make equally attractive containers and can be colour-matched to the plant materials. You can buy ozone-friendly cans of spray paint and get to work on baskets or any other container which may look a little faded or lack-lustre.

Baskets take well to bands of colour, such as vertical, horizontal or diagonal stripes of, say, heathery blue and crushed strawberry pink. Brilliant shades such as scarlet and buttercup yellow seem less appropriate. Old ceramic vases, discarded teapots, coffee mugs and many other household items can be brought into decorative service with a splash of paint. And for one of the techniques, spatter-painting, splash is the word. Paint the container with one colour, it could be cornflower blue, and allow it to dry, then spatter it with short bursts of a second colour, when it will look as if it has been caught in a shower of coloured rain. Ragwork is another technique which looks well on ceramic or other containers. Paint the surface with one colour – it could be pink to match larkspur or rosebuds – and dab it with a small piece of plastic sponge to give it a textured effect.

Gradually, as you build up a collection of dried materials, holding material and other aids, and a variety of containers, you will have all it takes to create designs for your home and for special occasions, the designs we explore in the following chapters.

BELOW
This delightful basket arrangement of peonies, rosebuds, strawflowers and sea lavender cleverly conceals the vital mechanics – crumpled chicken wire held firmly in place with strips of adhesive tape.

PEACHES AND CREAM

YOU WILL NEED:

BULBOUS VASE

CHICKEN WIRE

FLORISTS' ADHESIVE TAPE

—

PEONIES

APRICOT STATICE

SEA HOLLY

APRICOT STRAWFLOWERS

BLUE LARKSPUR

1 *The vase is fitted with crumpled chicken wire secured with florists' adhesive tape.*

2 *A bunch of pale peach peonies, towering high above the dried furled foliage, forms the foundation of this tall, traditional design.*

3 *More peonies are positioned to give weight toward the base of the arrangement. Statice, in a deeper colour tone, begins to fill in the spaces.*

4 *The dull, bluish grey of the sea holly, neutral in its colour effect, serves to emphasize the soft peaches and cream tones. Strawflowers provide smaller circles of the key colour.*

5 *Spikes of deep blue larkspur are used as strong colour pointers; they are carefully positioned to conceal many of the tall peony stems.*

DECORATING WITH DRIED FLOWERS

CHAPTER THREE
Arrangements Around the Home

L ARKSPUR AND LAVENDER, STRAW-
flowers and statice, exciting colours
and exotic seedheads – florists and
department stores have an ever-increasing
display of dried flowers and other plant
materials. While you are gradually building
up your collection of your own dried and
preserved flowers and leaves, you can
supplement it with commercially dried – and
often dyed – materials in an inspiring range
of colours.

Dyed seedheads and grasses can greatly
extend the colour span of your collection but
be sure, before you buy them, that they will
harmonize with your existing stock. Some
of the more vibrant colours do not look at all
natural, and can dominate any group. Hold
bunches of flowers and grasses in your hand,
half-close your eyes and assess the effect of
the tapestry of colour. If one bunch seems to
strike a jarring note, exchange it for another
until you have a selection that you know will
look right in your home.

Enhance your collection, too, with
unusual and exotic materials from overseas.
Lotus flower seedheads, their trumpet
shapes full of holes; luffa (loofah) seedpods
with their chestnut-brown colouring and
ridged texture; plumosum heads with their
untidy spiky appearance; protea flowers in
various stages of development; jhuta, their
open pods like carved wooden flowers –
these materials in neutral shades and warm
rich browns blend well with home-spun
seedheads, with cones and nuts, and with
spices like cinnamon quills and nutmeg.
Buying these 'exotics', as florists call them,
need not break the bank. You can buy them
gradually, a few at a time, confident that
with careful handling they will last
indefinitely, a once-in-a-lifetime investment.

SIZING UP THE BACKGROUND

Before creating a dried flower arrangement,
consider carefully the background against
which it will be seen. Dried flower designs
take a little time and patience to compose
and will give you pleasure for many months
to come, and so it is important that they are
at one with their surroundings.

Look at each room critically and consider
whether a lasting flower arrangement should
provide a highlight of colour or should blend
in with the furnishings. If a room is
furnished in neutral shades of cream and
brown it may be that a design in tones of,
say, orange and yellow or blue and purple
may be just what it needs to bring the
scheme to life. A basket of golden statice
bunches in the hearth or a blue and white jug
of purple statice on a table would become the
focal point of the room, a sharp, attention-
seeking accent of colour.

There may be a secondary colour in the
room which could be accentuated in your
choice of flowers. Perhaps the curtains or
wallpaper have a hint of pale pink that gives
a cue for a floral design in the same hue. A
deeper or brighter shade of pink picked up in
the flowers would create a pleasant

A TAPESTRY OF COLOUR

YOU WILL NEED:

TALL VASE OR JUG

CHICKEN WIRE

FLORISTS' ADHESIVE TAPE

—

BLUE LARKSPUR

MAUVE STATICE

RED ROSEBUDS

RED MINIATURE ROSES

DRIED PURPLE SAGE LEAVES

1 *The neck of the blue and white jug is filled with a mound of crumpled chicken wire held in place by florists' adhesive tape.*

2 *With the tallest stems at the centre and the shortest ones at the side, the blue larkspur is arranged to form a rough fan shape.*

3 *The statice is arranged among the larkspur to add deep blocks of colour.*

4 *Some extending almost to the uppermost tip and others angled low over the container rim, the roses distribute their colour brightness evenly throughout the design.*

5 *In such a rich tapestry of colour, the neutral tone of the dried sage leaves strikes the perfect balance. Notice how the leaves are placed not only at the base but on each side of the design.*

harmony. It may be that a country-style blend of cream and pink strawflowers and larkspur, pink gypsophila and brighter pink sunray (swan river) everlastings would look tailor-made for the room. Or perhaps a mass of flowers of a single type – bunches of strawflowers in varying shades of pink – would create a more eye-catching display.

If the room – a hall, perhaps – is furnished in black, white and grey, an elegant and uncompromising scheme, flowers in a primary colour may be needed to hold the attention. Pinks and pale blues, soft yellows and mauves would all look faded and bleached against the stark contrast of the surroundings. Go for flowers in bright red, sunshine yellow or strident blue. You could choose a jug of brilliant red peonies, their colour commanding attention from every angle, or a bowl of deep red roses to strike a slightly softer note. You could arrange statice in the sharpest tones of yellow with pure white gypsophila or lacy sea lavender for a slightly veiled effect or, more simply, place a pot of yellow tansy where it will make the strongest impression. In the blue theme, you could arrange a tall white jug of blue and white larkspur or a bright blue jug of pure white dried flowers, a blend of different shapes, sizes and textures that would harmonize perfectly with the room scheme. The use of colour and the relationship of one colour to another is explained more fully in The Colour Wheel panel on pages 48 to 49.

Important as colour is in creating harmonious effects, it is not the only consideration when planning a significant flower arrangement for a room. The size and scale of any patterned furnishings has to be taken into account when choosing the flowers, the container and the style of the design. Depending on the complexity or otherwise of the furnishings, a flower arrangement may blend so discreetly with the background as to be almost unnoticeable, or it may stand out boldly, becoming the focal point of the room.

If the walls and curtains are plain or textured, there are no limitations on the

FLOWER SHAPES

There are three basic shapes among the whole beautiful range of dried flowers and, in a mixed display, it is effective to include them all.

● First and foremost, and by far the largest group, are the full, round flowers such as strawflowers, roses, peonies and mop-headed hydrangeas and, among the seedheads, onion, poppy, globe thistle and carline thistle. These are the shapes to arrange at the heart of a design and close to the centre base, where they will become the focal point.

● Next there are the sprays, of statice, lavender, larkspur and astilbe (spirea), dock, love-lies-bleeding and many others. These materials, with their straight stems and spiky characteristics, are the ones to define the height and width of a design, to draw the outlines and feature in the extremities.

● And then there are the flowers and grasses with lacy shapes that give a soft, veiled effect to an arrangement and blur harsher outlines. These include sea lavender, gypsophila and lady's mantle, miniature everlasting (Pithocarpa corymbulosa), seacrest (Helichrysum cordatum), pampas and other grasses.

A design which draws freely from these three groups will have heightened interest, and be rich in texture. When the flowers and seedheads are in a limited colour range, the accent on the texture is strengthened and the contrasting shapes become, apparently, more pronounced.

designs you can create to display there. A basket of dried flowers arranged singly will have all the charm of a mixed herbaceous border in summer, and every flower will be seen to its full advantage.

If, on the other hand, the background against which the arrangement is seen has a bold or busy pattern, the same basket may look fussy and cluttered, and not at all at home in its environment. In these

THE COLOUR WHEEL

If you have ever wondered why blue and orange flowers make such a perfect partnership, each bloom bringing out the best in its neighbour, or why red flowers look at their most vibrant when arranged with green foliage, the answer is to be found in the colour wheel. This is an arrangement of colours, in the order in which they appear in the rainbow, which enables you to tell at a glance which colours are complementary and which ones are harmonious.

● To make a colour wheel, draw circles and divide them into six equal segments. Colour or write in the three primary colours – blue, yellow and red – in three alternate spaces around the outer wheel. Primary colours are the ones that cannot be made by mixing other colours together. (See Wheel 1.)

● Between the primary colours are the secondary ones, made by mixing together the colours on either side. This places green between blue and yellow, orange between yellow and red and mauve between red and blue. (See Wheel 1.)

● The most complementary colours are the ones facing each other on the wheel: the attraction of opposites – blue cornflowers and orange lilies, or blue flowers seen against an orange background; yellow daffodils and mauve irises; red roses and green nicotiana, or red flowers placed against a green wall. These are the combinations to go for to achieve the most eye-catching and strident effects. (See Wheel 2.)

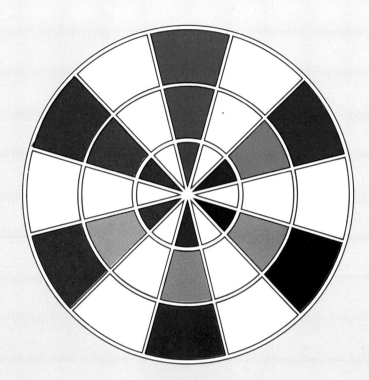

WHEEL 1: PRIMARY AND SECONDARY COLOURS;
TINTS AND TONES

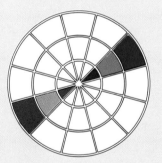

WHEEL 2: COMPLEMENTARY COLOURS

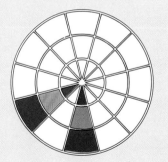

WHEEL 3: HARMONIOUS COLOURS

- *Harmonious colours, ones which blend well together for a more subtle effect, are those next to each other on the wheel: blue and green, or yellow, orange and red (See Wheel 3). Create a design in these colour combinations and no single flower or flower colour will stand out, or be seen to such full effect.*

- *Colours also have the ability to deceive the eye – a useful ploy in flower arranging. 'Cool' colours such as blue and green seem further away, while 'warm' colours such as red and orange seem closer than they are. Experiment for yourself when you are next composing a multi-coloured arrangement. Recess blue and green materials in the heart of the design and have the reds and oranges thrusting forwards. The effect will be to exaggerate the reality and give the design an enhanced dimension.*

- *Each of the six colours has a wide range of variables, not only the basic hue but all the tints, tones and shades that are so apparent in any selection of flowers. A tint is the basic hue mixed with white (see the middle band of Wheel 1). A tone is the basic colour mixed with grey (see inner band of Wheel 1), and a shade is the basic hue blended with black. For the most subtle and agreeable effects, you can arrange dried flowers in a single colour, but in several tints, tones and shades of that colour – a cluster of strawflowers for example, from palest pink through the middle tones to deepest red, or a bowl of mauve pansies and chive flowers, and purple marjoram set against a pale mauve background.*

circumstances it is better to compose an arrangement in a limited colour range, or one using large blocks of colour that will show up well against the pattern.

Designs in a single colour blended with cream or white or a range of tints from, say, palest pink to richest red put emphasis on the shape and texture of the flowers, and present an interesting challenge to the flower arranger.

If the background pattern of walls or curtains is small – it may be composed of small posies of flowers or a tracery of flowers and foliage – a dried flower display using well-defined blocks of colour would be more effective than one in which the materials are arranged singly. To achieve this effect you simply arrange the dried materials in bunches or clusters, not one pencil-slim side shoot of fluffy golden rod but several, wired together to form a sunshine yellow mass of colour; not one single pinky-peach strawflower creating a small pool of colour, but five or six, wired together and creating a real splash; not single feverfew flowers inserting snow-white polka dots among their more colourful neighbours, but ten or fifteen bunched together to form sizeable highlights which could become a focal point of the design. When dried materials are arranged in this way, in clusters rather than single units, the design has a far more pronounced colour impact and will be able to hold its own against even a multi-patterned background.

Another way to maximize the colour impact is to arrange flowers in blocks of colour. You might have a deep earthenware bowl and a medley of flowers in pink, blue, gold and cream. Instead of composing the arrangement so that the colours are evenly distributed throughout the design, try arranging them in rainbow blocks, all the pink ones in one quarter, all the blue ones in another, and so on. The visual effect is exciting, and very unusual. As a variation on this theme, you can arrange flowers in stripes according to their colour. You might have a rectangular basket fitted with a piece of crumpled wire-mesh netting and an

50

YOU WILL NEED:
WHITE PEDESTAL CONTAINER
BLOCK OF DRY FOAM
FLORISTS' ADHESIVE TAPE
—
GREEN PHALARIS
PINK LARKSPUR
LOVE-IN-A-MIST SEEDHEADS
PINK ROSEBUDS
GREEN OATS
GREEN-DYED SEA LAVENDER

1 *A block of dry foam, with the corners cut, just fits the white pottery pedestal container. It is held firmly in place with criss-crossed florists' adhesive tape.*

2 *This is a design which relies for effect on the abundance of the dried materials used. The phalaris is arranged first, in bunches of nine or ten stems.*

3 *The short stems of pink larkspur perfectly complement the soft, pale green of the phalaris.*

4 *A change of texture and shape. The purple and green striped love-in-a-mist seedheads are arranged to fill in the spaces, with some dipping low over the container rim.*

5 *The rosebud stems are cut to form a gentle dome shape with easy, elegant curves.*

6 *Wispy outlines soften the design without destroying the overall shape. They are contributed by oats and green-dyed sea lavender which fill the remaining spaces.*

51

armful of flowers in blue, white and yellow. Divide the flowers into their separate colours and arrange them blue, white, yellow, white across the basket for a modern look and a design that will stand up to the fiercest competition from furnishing patterns.

A dining table is an easy background for dried flower arrangements. Seen against the plain wood background even the smallest and most intricate designs show up well. Consider the colour tone of the wood and plan pastel and bright colours to contrast with a dark surface, or deeper tones to be silhouetted against pale wood. If you cover the table with a patterned cloth, even a heavy lace one, take this into consideration when planning the flower arrangements. All the rules about a bolder approach and using stronger colour blocks will apply.

CHOOSING CONTAINERS

When it comes to choosing containers for dried and preserved materials, it is a case of anything goes. A container does not need to be waterproof, does not need to contain an inner water-holding vessel, and does not even need to have an aperture. You can fix a saucer of foam to a tall candlestick and use it as a simulated pedestal, or fix dried flowers to a one-dimensional background such as a woven placemat or a flat hanging-basket shape to create a lively wall-hanging.

BASKETS

Baskets of all kinds have a special affinity with dried flowers and are likely to feature prominently in any enthusiast's collection of containers. Large, deep baskets to hold a vibrant display of dried flowers in a fireplace; round, deep shopping baskets to stand in a room corner; circular willow baskets to decorate a dining table; they all look tailor-made for dried flower displays.

Before making your choice of basket for any given situation, consider its size

carefully. If you are planning a fan-shaped arrangement with long spires of larkspur and clarkia angled away at each side, the finished design could be anything up to twice the width of the container. And it could be expensive in its use of dried materials.

One of the secrets of successful dried flower arranging is that the container should be packed with flowers, to give a look of luxury. It is far more effective to have a smaller container filled to overflowing with a generous display of dried materials than a larger one that looks sparse and unfinished. Not only that, when flowers are arranged to give a filled-in tapestry effect, the stems, be they wire, cane or natural, are completely hidden from view by the massed flowerheads. This is the look of a well-stocked garden in high summer, and is the effect to aim for in all dried flower designs.

You might have a large, flat basket with a looped handle or two side handles. One way to arrange it, using foam as the holding material, would be to position dried flower stems vertically, straight, soldierly stems of, say, wheat, lavender, roses and love-in-a-mist as erect as when they are growing. Another way, which heightens the interest, is to arrange several separate containers to stand in the basket. You might have a collection of small posy baskets, the kind you can buy cheaply at charity shops, a collection of pottery beakers, or several earthenware flower pots. Arrange each container with its own limited colour range of materials – cream and white in one, blue and cream in another – and stand the containers side by side in the basket. Displayed on a hall table, a chest of drawers or a sideboard, the basket would be full of interest and could become – as you rearrange the separate containers – a constantly changing display.

Small posy baskets make perfect individual containers for a dining table, arrangements that can be at the ready to decorate the most impromptu of lunch or dinner parties. Fill the aperture with crumpled wire-mesh netting and arrange nosegays of small dried flowers, side shoots

RAINBOW PALETTE

YOU WILL NEED:
BASKET
RAFFIA OR TWINE
—
SELECTION OF BLUE-DYED FLOWERS
SELECTION OF YELLOW FLOWERS
SELECTION OF GREEN-DYED FLOWERS AND GRASSES
SELECTION OF RED FLOWERS

1 *No fixing material is needed for this design. The flowers are tied into thick bundles of a single colour, the stems cut short so that the lowest flower heads just rest on the rim of the basket.*

2 *First the blue, then the yellow and now the pale green – the blocks of colour build up, each one complementing the other.*

3 *The finished design, with the four bunches of dyed and everlasting flowers in place. It is one of the simplest to create, and can be carried out with any combination of colours.*

and clippings. Small-scale materials of this kind may be left over from a large display in the room, and would in that case make a perfect match.

Baskets are as versatile as they are decorative. You can buy designs specially made to hang on the wall, with a flat back and a curved, pouched front to take a drooping, trailing, overhanging display of dried materials. Consider arranging a wall basket in rich autumnal tones of brown and gold, with trails of preserved hops and copper beech leaves, sprays of dried oak foliage, teasels, hogweed seedheads and brilliant clusters of tansy and golden rod. Or take a completely different approach and fill a rugged basket with a more delicate selection of pinks and blues, with preserved leaves and old-man's-beard to form a colour link. Hang a basket between two doors or windows, above a piece of furniture, on a door or on a little-used cupboard.

Narrow shoulder baskets make perfect wall-hangings, too. Fill one side of a basket with a diagonally placed sheaf of dried wheat, barley or oats, with an armful of dried grasses, or with bunches of dried statice, for a made-in-moments display that is every bit as eye-catching as an intricate arrangement. Or fill the aperture with a block or two of dried foam and create a fan shape of dried materials to hang over a chimney-piece or stand in the hearth.

Coloured baskets have a separate role to play. They can be colour-matched to any soft furnishings or decorating scheme, but seem especially appropriate in a bedroom. A basket sprayed in deep purple looks effective with pale pink peonies, purple marjoram and lavender, and could fill a room corner or stand on a chest of drawers. A painted posy basket filled with rosebuds would be pretty on a dressing-table, and a shoulder bag woven in coloured stripes could be filled with trailing flowers and hung on a bed post or door.

If you think that natural willow and other woven baskets are too rugged for your home, consider prettying them up in a number of ways. You can thread satin or lace ribbon through the upright spokes and finish it with a flourish, a generous bow with trailing ends, or bind the handle round and round with ribbon. You can line the edge of a basket with lacy white or gold doilies, the decorative edging overlapping the rim. And you can finish off a dried flower design with a sizeable bow of 'raffia' paper ribbon, chosen to match one of the prominent flower colours.

METAL CONTAINERS

The glint and gleam of metal adds a sparkle to dried materials that are, in the main, matt and lacking in sheen. A copper milk jug brimming over with a winter mixture of preserved leaves, golden rod, yellow achillea (yarrow), Chinese lanterns and fir cones: a pewter sugar bowl pretty as a picture with pink sunray (swan river) everlasting, pale pink clover and blue cornflowers; a silver christening mug with ice-cool gypsophila, silver-and-cream carline thistle, silver foliage and pink rosebuds; a brass preserving pan glittering in the hearth with a high-on-texture collection of bulrushes, dried mushrooms, moss and exotic seedheads; a galvanized bucket or watering can filled with bunches and bunches of multi-coloured statice and sea lavender – the partnerships are endless, and invariably sympathetic.

Since dried flower containers do not need to be waterproof, damaged finds in junk shops are entirely suitable. Keep a look out at car boot or garage sales, in charity shops and other bargain centres for metal containers of all kinds. Cream jugs, milk cans, beakers, goblets, troughs, boxes, tins, tea caddys and weighing scales all have a decorative potential in the eyes of an imaginative flower arranger.

To take full advantage of all its glitter potential, the metal should be well polished, and, after cleaning, rubbed with a soft cloth. If crumpled wire-mesh netting is used as a stem holder, the containers should be protected from scratches by a thick band of tape stuck around the inside of the rim, or by slivers cut from a block of foam.

JEWEL BOX

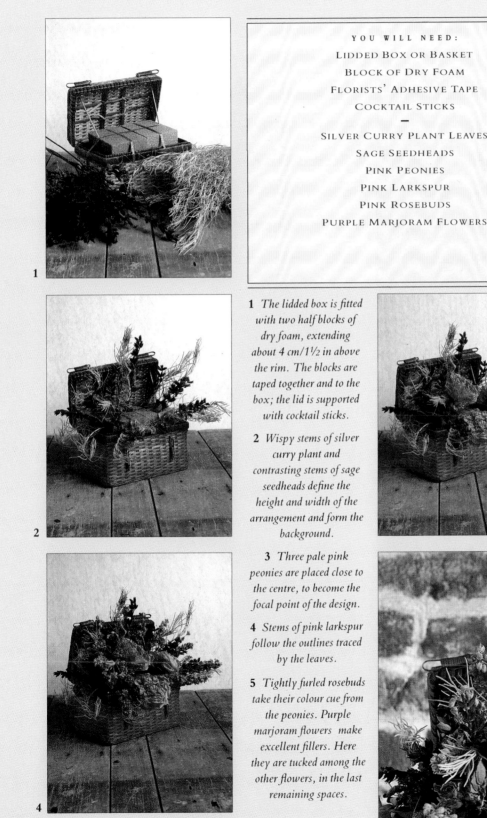

YOU WILL NEED:

LIDDED BOX OR BASKET
BLOCK OF DRY FOAM
FLORISTS' ADHESIVE TAPE
COCKTAIL STICKS
—
SILVER CURRY PLANT LEAVES
SAGE SEEDHEADS
PINK PEONIES
PINK LARKSPUR
PINK ROSEBUDS
PURPLE MARJORAM FLOWERS

1 *The lidded box is fitted with two half blocks of dry foam, extending about 4 cm/1½ in above the rim. The blocks are taped together and to the box; the lid is supported with cocktail sticks.*

2 *Wispy stems of silver curry plant and contrasting stems of sage seedheads define the height and width of the arrangement and form the background.*

3 *Three pale pink peonies are placed close to the centre, to become the focal point of the design.*

4 *Stems of pink larkspur follow the outlines traced by the leaves.*

5 *Tightly furled rosebuds take their colour cue from the peonies. Purple marjoram flowers make excellent fillers. Here they are tucked among the other flowers, in the last remaining spaces.*

AUTUMN GLORY

YOU WILL NEED:
WALL-HANGING BASKET
2 BLOCKS OF DRY FOAM
FLORISTS' ADHESIVE TAPE
—
PRESERVED LEAVES
HOGWEED SEEDHEADS
TEASELS
CHINESE LANTERNS
ORANGE-DYED ACHILLEA (YARROW)
OATS
PRESERVED BELLS-OF-IRELAND

1 *The wall-hanging basket, made of woven dried leaves, is wedged with two blocks of dry foam taped together with florists' adhesive tape. As the foam fits tightly, no fixing materials are necessary.*

2 *Sprays of preserved leaves are arranged to form a cross shape. The hogweed seedheads form the centre of the design.*

3 *Teasels with their solid oval shapes and soft neutral colouring, begin to fill in the arrangement, their heads outlining a rough triangle.*

4 *Curving stems of Chinese lanterns, with some of the seedheads still at the pale green stage, follow the lower outlines. Orange-dyed achillea (yarrow), forming solid blocks of colour, fill in the centre.*

5

5 *A few wispy stems of
oats are added at the sides
and in the centre. Bells-
of-Ireland, the stems cut
short, are placed to fill
in the spaces and
complement the strong
orange colouring.*

COLOURFUL CAULDRON

YOU WILL NEED:
LARGE METAL CONTAINER
CHICKEN WIRE
—
PINK LARKSPUR
WHITE STATICE
APRICOT STATICE
YELLOW STATICE
BLUE STATICE
WHITE SEA LAVENDER

1 The neck of the cauldron is filled with crumpled chicken wire, wedged under the rim. Pink larkspur is arranged in a fan shape.

2 Stems of white statice, which will form a neutral element in the design, are positioned among the larkspur.

3 The apricot statice is mingled with the pink larkspur in the foreground, while the yellow and blue forms are arranged in blocks of a single colour.

4 More white statice is added to dilute the strident effect of the brilliant yellow, and white sea lavender outlines the design like a lace collar.

PORCELAIN, CHINA AND POTTERY CONTAINERS

Pieces of porcelain, china and pottery have a slightly limited appeal as dried flower containers. Those with an intricate or delicate pattern can seem at odds with the dried materials, and need to be used with care. A rose-patterned teapot, for example, may look prettier when arranged with a bunch of roses than with a mixed and more complex medley of several flower types. A blue-and-white ginger jar may look more effective when arranged with a flourish of white or blue flowers than with mixed colours. A modern pottery bowl richly patterned with splashes of primary colours is best arranged with flowers echoing a single colour, or with neutral tones of cream or white.

One of the most effective of china containers is a white pedestal vase, which you can often find in second-hand shops. It lifts the flowers high off the table surface and heightens the interest factor. You could arrange such a container with dyed glixia (star flower), green grasses, gypsophila and roses. When you are cutting rose stems short to arrange them close to the foam there is no need to waste the dried leaves. Cut them from the stems, wire them together in clusters and insert them among the flowers for a refreshingly natural look.

Glazed and unglazed pottery in all the earthy brown and green shades is a perfect foil for dried flowers and other materials. A tall jug arranged with bulrushes and teasels looks well on a hall table. A beaker brimming over with decorative grasses is a perfect decoration for a kitchen and a flower pot fanning out with a mixture of brown, cream and golden tones is an appropriate display for a hearth or covered porch.

GLASS CONTAINERS

Some of the prettiest dried flower containers around are made of coloured glass; they may be bowls, beakers, mugs, drinking glasses or vases. Opaque glass has the advantage that it hides the plant stems and does not need camouflage tactics such as a lining of moss or pot-pourri (see page 42). The reflective glass, like metal, is flattering to the matt appearance of dried flowers. Careful colour co-ordination is essential if the flowers and container are to look completely unified, and one flower type should echo the colour of the glass as accurately as possible. A group of three red trumpet-shaped glasses arranged with vibrant everlastings as a table centrepiece; a blue and green petal vase arranged with bells-of-Ireland and cornflowers for a dressing-table – coloured glass and dried flowers have an especially decorative relationship.

WOODEN CONTAINERS

Wooden containers have a wide application in dried flower design. You can use salad bowls, bread boards, cheese boards, a slice across a tree trunk, beakers, tankards, cutlery trays and lidded boxes, plant trays, garden trugs, plant troughs and hollowed logs for a wide range of designs to display all around the house. The wood may be polished or unpolished, sun-bleached and faded or painted. Whatever the finish, wooden containers take well to a mixed display of dried flowers. A mahogany teabox, for example, its lid propped open, looks luxurious with the aperture brimming with a tumbling display of buttercups, roses, clarkia, marjoram, hydrangea and lady's mantle – a rich-looking medley in jewel colours. A hollowed log makes a perfect container for a porch or sun-room, the top wedged with a block of foam and arranged with, say, bunches of statice, wheat, golden rod and sea lavender. And a wooden bread board makes a perfect base for an upright design composed in a hidden plastic saucer of foam. The arrangement could have a candle as a focal point, with fir cones, reed mace seedheads, lotus flower seedheads, skeletonized leaves and pressed autumn leaves to give a textural balance. For a festive occasion, the materials could be spatter-sprayed with gold paint.

CHINESE YELLOW

YOU WILL NEED:
CHINA OR POTTERY BOWL
BLOCK DRY FOAM
FLORISTS' ADHESIVE TAPE
—
BLUE PRESERVED EUCALYPTUS LEAVES
CREAM STRAWFLOWERS
BLUE CORNFLOWERS
GOLDEN STRAWFLOWERS
YELLOW ACHILLEA (YARROW)
BLUE SEA HOLLY

1 *The blue and white china bowl is fitted with a trimmed block of dry foam taped from side to side with florists' adhesive tape.*

2 *Blue preserved eucalyptus forms the basis of the design. Some of the stems are cut short so that the leaves nestle close against the foam and help conceal it.*

3 *Cream strawflowers, contrasting strikingly with the eucalyptus in every way, are recessed into the design. The bright deep blue of the cornflowers echoes the colour of the bowl.*

4 *The golden strawflowers with their intense colouring, give an Oriental look to the design. They are positioned to increase the height of the flower dome beneath the outline of the leaves.*

5

5 *The flat flowerheads of
the yellow achillea
(yarrow) and the
indefinite outlines of the
misty blue sea holly add
to the textural interest of
the design while keeping
within the two-colour
scheme.*

CANDLE POWER

YOU WILL NEED:
RECTANGULAR, PLASTIC FOAM HOLDER
PIECE OF DRY FOAM
PLASTIC CANDLE SPIKE
CANDLE
—
PINK STATICE
MAUVE STATICE
WHITE SEA LAVENDER
YELLOW ROSES

1 *The rectangular plastic holder takes a slice cut from a large block of dry foam. The candle spike is inserted in the centre.*

2 *Stems of pink and mauve statice blend together to create a rich colour effect. The side stems are cut short and the flowerheads pressed close against the foam.*

3 *As more statice is added, long stems at the ends, short ones at the sides, the colour intensifies.*

4 *Sprays of wispy white sea lavender are pressed into the foam between the tightly packed statice, lightening the overall effect.*

5 *A handful of yellow roses are positioned to stand erect, rising high above the colourful mound of statice and sea lavender.*

CANDLE TIP

There are two ways of inserting a candle into foam without breaking up the holding material. One is to use a purpose-made plastic spike, available from florists. The other is to tape four matchsticks or wooden cocktail sticks around the base of the candle, with the slivers of wood extending about 2cm/¾in below the candle. Push the matchsticks into the foam and the candle will rest on top of it, without making a hole.

CARING FOR YOUR ARRANGEMENTS

Dried flower arrangements will give you pleasure for many months or even years as long as they are kept in favourable conditions. As we have seen, they will not tolerate excessive dampness in the atmosphere – they reabsorb moisture and soon go mouldy – and so steamy kitchens and bathrooms are out of bounds to all except the hardiest of seedheads.

Strong light is the other enemy. Dried flowers look enchanting in a sunny windowsill catching every shaft of the warm southern sun. But the sun is of short-lived benefit, and will soon draw out the colour from the flowers and fade them, pinks and blues alike, to a standard pale cream.

For this reason it is advisable to place dried flower designs in a part of the room that does not catch direct sunlight. If this happens to be a dark corner of the room, select flowers in pale colours – soft yellows, pinks and cream – that will show up well, and gleam with all the intensity of a table lamp.

When in the fullness of time you may tire of a flower arrangement and feel in need of a change, or when you start lighting fires and make the fireplace display redundant, you can take the design apart and re-use the materials. Dismantle the arrangement carefully, stem by stem, and ruthlessly discard any faded or damaged flowers. Cut off any florets or leaves that have been squashed or broken and generally trim and tidy up stems. Store the remaining 'good' flowers between tissues in a box, or standing upright in a container until you are ready to use them again.

If a flower arrangement begins to look rather dusty and lacks its original personality, take it to an open window and, very gently, blow off the dust using a hair dryer on the coolest, slowest setting. Appraise the arrangement for any signs of fading, and replace any stems which have lost their colour. It might amount to only half a dozen new flowers, but these could make all the difference, prolonging the life of the arrangement for several months to come.

AIRTIGHT ARRANGEMENTS FOR BATHROOMS

Dried flowers do not like a steamy atmosphere, and will survive in a bathroom only if it is well ventilated. In a room that suffers from high humidity you can overcome the problem by placing the flowers in an airtight container.

- *Choose a clear, glass-lidded storage jar and place a cardboard tube inside it. Push dried strawflower heads into the cavity between the tube and the glass, arranging them in neat rings of different colours. Finish with one large flower on top of the tube, put on the lid and tie a ribbon round the neck of the jar.*

- *Alternatively, cut a cardboard circle to fit the base of a wide-necked jar. Press a blob of adhesive clay on to it and arrange an elongated design of flowers and foliage, taking care to conceal the holding material. Lower the arrangement into the jar and put the lid on a design that is now steamproof.*

BROWN STUDY

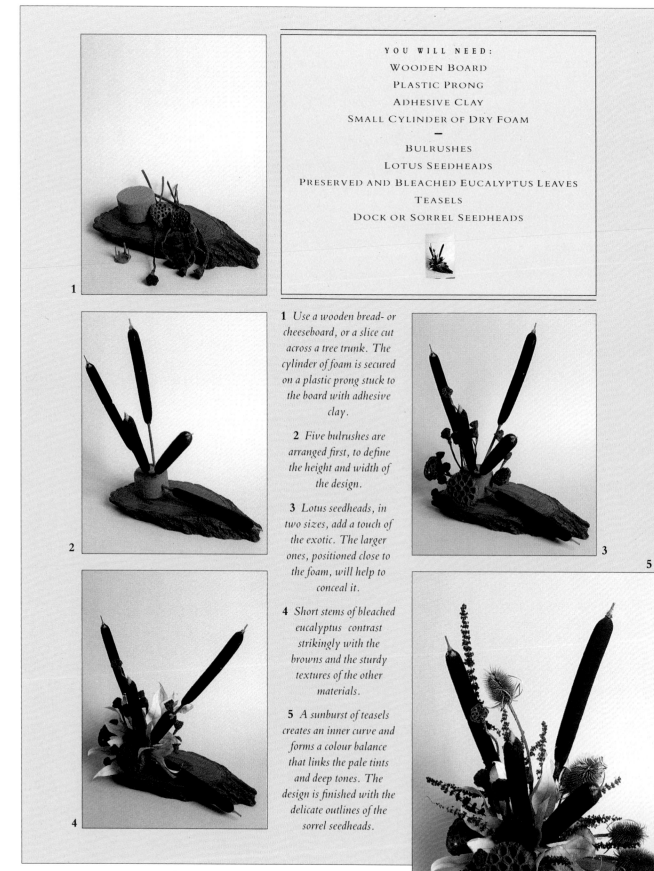

YOU WILL NEED:
WOODEN BOARD
PLASTIC PRONG
ADHESIVE CLAY
SMALL CYLINDER OF DRY FOAM
—
BULRUSHES
LOTUS SEEDHEADS
PRESERVED AND BLEACHED EUCALYPTUS LEAVES
TEASELS
DOCK OR SORREL SEEDHEADS

1 *Use a wooden bread- or cheeseboard, or a slice cut across a tree trunk. The cylinder of foam is secured on a plastic prong stuck to the board with adhesive clay.*

2 *Five bulrushes are arranged first, to define the height and width of the design.*

3 *Lotus seedheads, in two sizes, add a touch of the exotic. The larger ones, positioned close to the foam, will help to conceal it.*

4 *Short stems of bleached eucalyptus contrast strikingly with the browns and the sturdy textures of the other materials.*

5 *A sunburst of teasels creates an inner curve and forms a colour balance that links the pale tints and deep tones. The design is finished with the delicate outlines of the sorrel seedheads.*

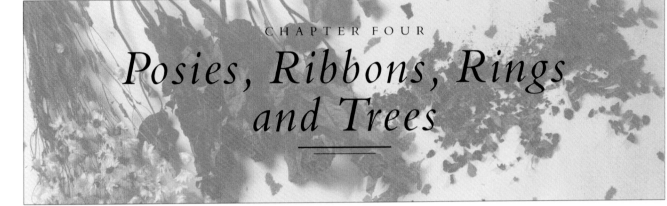

CHAPTER FOUR

Posies, Ribbons, Rings and Trees

D RIED FLOWERS LEND THEMSELVES TO designs in all kinds of shapes, from a bridal posy to a garland to decorate the church; from a flourish on an Easter bonnet to a festive centrepiece for the table, from an indoor designer tree to a swag draped across a fireplace. Some of these designs are composed of flowers and foliage alone; others are constructed on the preformed foam shapes sold by many florists. They are all intensely pretty, and long-lasting, a special joy when they are created to celebrate a romantic occasion.

POSIES

Posies come in all shapes and sizes and have many applications. There is the Victorian-style posy composed of a number of concentric rings around a central flower, usually a perfect rosebud. Such posies have all the romantic associations and nostalgia that makes them the perfect choice for a wedding day. Others are less formally arranged, the flowers cascading in a free-fall way, with no clearly defined shape, just an overall attractive outline. Some dried flower posies, small and dainty, are made to be worn on a dress or suit for a special occasion, and others are designed to provide a finishing touch to a favourite hat or an Easter bonnet. The flower-bedecked hat may be worn with style, or it may be hung on a door or in a hallway, or placed as a decoration on the bed.

Some posies are designed to take the place of flower arrangements in the home; most of all the flat-on-one-side posies that are constructed flower by flower on a working surface. Such posies can be placed on a low piece of furniture – a coffee table is ideal, since it is always viewed from above – or on a wide windowsill, though not a south-facing one. They are equally effective as wall decorations, hanging between two doors or windows, in an alcove or on a door. You may even find an unusual vehicle for them, such as a grass broom.

Other posies are designed to hang on furniture and furnishings. A nosegay of rosebuds, lady's mantle, sea lavender and larkspur would look enchanting hanging from a bedpost or on the back of a Windsor chair, on a wardrobe door handle or on a curtain tie-back.

Victorian-style posies represent the most formal designs of the group and call for the most meticulous attention to detail. Just one flower straying from the pattern of perfect circles can spoil the design. If such a posy is created for display in a vase it can usually be composed of dried flowers on their natural stems. But if it is to be carried, each flower should be wired on to a false stem and taped with gutta-percha. The cluster of woody and brittle stems would be difficult to present elegantly, and cumbersome to hold.

Choose some flowers which are small and round, such as rosebuds, cornflowers, strawflowers, sunray (swan river) everlasting, scabious and marigolds, some small seedheads for a variety of texture –

VICTORIAN POSIES

1 *A romantic set of pink and white cup, saucer, and jug is all ready to hold a pretty bedroom design. The cup is fitted with crumpled chicken wire held in place with two strips of florists' adhesive tape.*

2 *The cup is arranged with a fragrant nosegay of lavender and larkspur, the stems positioned to form a gentle mound.*

3 *The posy for the jug is composed in the hand: a pink rosebud in the centre, then a ring of phalaris and a collar of gypsophila. Rosebuds and love-in-a-mist seedheads alternate to form the outer ring. At this stage, the stems are bound with a stub wire.*

4 *The layers of the posy are built up, with more rosebuds, love-in-a-mist seedheads and green oats added to form a concentric and tightly packed design.*

5 *Slender stems of white and green-dyed sea lavender outline the posy, resembling the delicate lace collar that was a feature of Victorian designs.*

YOU WILL NEED:

CHINA CUP AND SAUCER

CHINA JUG

CHICKEN WIRE

FLORISTS' ADHESIVE TAPE

MEDIUM-GAUGE STUB WIRES

—

LAVENDER

PINK LARKSPUR

PINK ROSEBUDS

GREEN PHALARIS

GYPSOPHILA

LOVE-IN-A-MIST SEEDHEADS

GREEN OATS

WHITE AND GREEN-DYED SEA LAVENDER

66

1

2

4

3

5

6

6 *A posy in one container, a burst of fragrant stems in the other – the designs would look attractive on a bedside table, a dressing table or a bedroom windowsill.*

EASTER BASKET

YOU WILL NEED:

MEDIUM-GAUGE STUB WIRES

EGGS

SHALLOW BASKET

—

SPHAGNUM MOSS

PINK RHODANTHE

PINK SEA LAVENDER

POPPY SEEDHEADS

PURPLE MARJORAM FLOWERS

LAVENDER

PINK STRAWFLOWERS

1 *The basket is filled with moss, a safe nest for the eggs.*

2 *A posy composed of pink rhodanthe, pink sea lavender and strawflowers. The stems are bound with a stub wire.*

3 *Two of the posies — they need not be identical — are attached to the basket rim, the ends of the stub wires pressed between the woven slats. The head of one posy covers and conceals the stems of the one before.*

4 *The basket rim is covered with a ring of posies, the round shapes of the everlasting flowers contrasting effectively with the lace-like stems of sea lavender.*

5 *When it is filled with eggs, the basket makes an eye-catching centrepiece for the Easter table.*

poppy and love-in-a-mist are ideal – and some contrasting flower shapes to edge the concentric rings – lily-of-the-valley or gypsophila, for example. Select some dried or preserved foliage to edge the posy and, in the traditional way, protect the flowers. This could be sage or purple sage, fennel or fern. Mount all the flowers and leaves on stub wires as explained on page 35.

To make the posy, hold the central flower, a golden rosebud perhaps, in one hand and arrange a ring of flowers around it. Gently bend the wire stems to ease the flowers into position, making sure that they are evenly spaced around the feature flower. Arrange another ring and then another, building up a design of perfect circles. Arrange the foliage evenly around the last ring and bind the cluster of wire stems together. Then, if you wish, push the posy stems through a hole cut in the centre of a paper doily and pleat it evenly all around. Secure the doily in place with adhesive tape. Bind the stems with satin ribbon, tied into a generous bow with long trailing ends.

A romantic posy like this is pretty for a bride or bridesmaid to carry, and would provide a lasting memento of the wedding day. It would also be suitable to present to a visiting guest speaker or honoured guest at a speech day or public function. Placed in a plain glass or china container, it would then make a permanent decoration for a dressing-table or chest of drawers.

The prettiest free-style posies are ones that draw their components from all three groups of flower shapes, spiky, round and lacy, as described on page 47. Think of a posy as a flower arrangement without a container and you will see that the long spires – they may be wheat, or dock, or clarkia – outline the design and draw in the extremities. The full, round flowers – they may be roses or strawflowers – provide weight at the heart of the design, close to the handle, and the lacy materials – lady's mantle or gypsophila, for example – provide a softening influence.

Gather together the materials and arrange and rearrange them in your hand until the design looks pleasing and balanced. Bind the

stems with wire and disguise it with a ribbon bow or one made of raffia paper ribbon, a material that is specially suited to enhance dried flower designs. Fix a fine wire loop to hang the posy on the wall or on a piece of furniture, on the corner of a mirror or a picture frame. Such designs are specially suited to a bedroom or spare bedroom.

DECORATING HATS

Hats of all kinds – straw boaters, wide-brimmed straw hats, white linen summer hats and elegant milliners' creations – are perfect candidates for dried flower decorations. It does not matter whether you intend to wear the hat for a special occasion or use it as a furnishing accessory, the result will be equally effective. A straw boater looks infinitely more festive with a hoop of dried flowers tacked to the ribbon band. Sea lavender and multi-coloured strawflowers give the hat a young and carefree look. For a slightly more formal effect you could compose a simple posy of, for example, a bright pink peony, a cluster of pink sunray (swan river) everlasting and a few sprays of gypsophila. A wide-brimmed straw hat looks stunning with a single flower or a bunch of flowers pinning back the brim at the front – one perfect dried rose or a bunch of rosebuds perhaps. In summer, white on white looks high fashion; a white lily and white sunray (swan river) everlasting would make a stunning decoration on a linen hat, and dried lilies or orchids would add style to an elegant creation to wear to a wedding. It is reassuring to know, on an occasion like that, that the flowers will stay in perfect condition all day long.

SWAGS AND RIBBONS

Dried flowers and other plant materials compose well into swags, plaits and ribbons to decorate a wall, pelmet or fireplace, the

PRESENTATION BOUQUET

YOU WILL NEED:

TWINE

RUST PAPER RIBBON

—

PAMPAS GRASS

GREEN OATS

GREEN WHEAT

CARTHAMUS

PALE PINK PEONIES

ORANGE STRAWFLOWERS

GREEN-DYED SEA LAVENDER

1 *The bouquet is arranged flat on a table surface, each layer placed on top of the one before. Three stems of pampas grass are placed first, to form the base of the design.*

2 *Long stems of green oats and wheat are arranged on top of the pampas grass, almost covering it completely. The stalks are gathered inwards at the base.*

3 *Long stems of green carthamus, still with their orange flowers, cover the oats and wheat. The heart of the design is formed with three full-petalled peonies which are placed close together and close to the top.*

4 *Long stems of orange strawflowers are tucked beneath the peonies, and others are arranged in graduated lengths along the spray. More green oats are placed over the flowers, giving a country look to the collection.*

5

5 *Sprays of green-dyed sea lavender are placed close to the 'handle', covering some of the clustered stems. Stems are tighly bound with twine and tied with a paper ribbon bow.*

fall of a buffet tablecloth or, for a wedding or christening, the screen or a pillar in church. Whether it is a raffia plait studded with bunches of wheat, cinnamon quills, nuts and nutmegs to hang in the kitchen, or a garland of evergreens studded with strawflowers to decorate a church, the designs are simple to make; they just need time and patience.

Swags and ribbons have long historical associations, deriving from the time when people used to garland the temples in celebration of a feast day. Centuries later, the tradition is gaining in popularity again as people make long-lasting swags to decorate their homes, or evergreen and dried flower designs in honour of a festive occasion.

The core of a garland or swag may be composed of a number of materials; which one you use may depend on the degree of permanency you wish the design to have, and on the nature of the design.

Simplest of all is a design known as a harvest plait, though it can be enjoyed throughout the year and is equally appropriate as a Christmas decoration. The core, or background, is a raffia plait of the kind you can buy in some florists or on market stalls, a thick, generous, bulging plait that needs little adornment to turn it into a stunning decoration. As an alternative, you can ask a friendly storekeeper to save you the plait used to hang a string of garlic, or you can make one yourself from thickly plaited raffia or even string.

For the decoration you can choose a selection of kitchen-orientated materials, including wheat, marjoram flowers, spices and small rosy apples; a colourful array of Chinese lanterns, brilliant strawflowers and pine cones; or a more subtle collection of dried flowers including rosebuds, perhaps, achillea (yarrow) and ornamental grasses.

Since wall decorations are likely to be viewed at a distance, it is best to use the dried materials in bunches and clusters rather than as single units. Wire several flowers or stems of a single type together, or make up mixed posies and wire them on to the plait. Whether you cover the plait completely, or leave a little of the high-texture background

to show through, is a matter of choice. Finish the design with a satin ribbon or raffia ribbon bow. Hang the plait on a door or between two doors or windows; hang a pair of plaits on either side of a fireplace, a door, a window or a bed, or to outline an alcove.

Other swags and ribbons are constructed on bases or cores that are solely functional and must be concealed by the decorative materials. The most substantial of these is a core made of rolled wire-mesh netting enclosing a roll of sphagnum moss, hay, or off-cuts of dry foam; a stout and sturdy centre for a permanent decoration. To make one of this type, measure the area to be decorated and cut a piece of netting to that length. Tease out the moss or hay to make a sausage shape along one edge of the wire, and roll up the wire tightly to enclose it. With a firm foundation like this, it is a simple – though time-consuming – matter to wire on bunches of dried materials until the core is completely hidden. You might choose sprays of dried or preserved leaves, bunches of wheat or barley heads, and a colourful medley of dried flowers.

For a less substantial core and one that is more suited to long garlands and ribbons you can use a length of stout cord or rope, covering it first with preserved leaves – for a long-lasting decoration – or evergreens, and then with ornamental clusters of flowers. This is the kind of floral ribbon to hang in loops over a fireplace (keeping it well away from the fire), over a door, a pelmet or an arch, across a screen in church, or to wind around a pillar.

CIRCLETS AND RINGS

Hoops and wreaths, circlets and rings, call them what you will, these designs make beautiful all-year-round decorations for the home, and spectacular ornaments for Christmas and other festivals. A pretty circlet hanging above a bedhead; a harvest ring to decorate the church for the festival; an Advent ring decorated with dried flowers

HARVEST PLAIT

YOU WILL NEED:

THICK RAFFIA PLAIT

MEDIUM-GAUGE STUB WIRES

RAFFIA

ADHESIVE CLAY

GOLD SPRAY PAINT

NARROW GREEN RIBBON

—

GOLDEN WHEAT

CONES

CINNAMON QUILLS

PECANS

WALNUTS

1 *The base of the wall decoration is a thick plait of raffia, which you can buy from florists. Bunches of wheat are bound with wire, and the ends pressed into the plait.*

2 *More wheat is added, in overlapping bunches, to cover the plait.*

3 *Stub wires cut in half are wrapped around the base of the cones. The bunches of cinnamon are wired, too, and then tied with raffia. The wire ends are pushed firmly into the plait.*

4 *Dabs of adhesive clay are pressed on to one side of the pecans and walnuts, and half a stub wire, bent into a hair pin shape, is pressed into each dab of clay. The nuts can be sprayed with gold. The plait is finished with ribbon bows.*

FLORAL RING

YOU WILL NEED:
DRY FOAM RING
—

PINK HYDRANGEA
PINK LARKSPUR
PINK ROSEBUDS
CREAM STRAWFLOWERS
PINK STRAWFLOWERS
LADY'S MANTLE

1 *A head of dried pink hydrangea is cut into clusters of florets and the stems pressed into the dry foam ring on all sides.*

2 *One stem of pink larkspur can be cut into three or four short lengths to furnish this design. The colour and the contrasting textures should be evenly distributed.*

3 *Rosebuds and strawflowers, the stems cut short and the flowers pressed close against the ring, fill in the design. Take care that the inside and outside of the ring is completely concealed.*

4 *Sprays of lime green lady's mantle add a delicate touch to this pretty, feminine design.*

5

5 *The ring can be
displayed flat on a table,
as here. If displayed on a
wall, attach a wire to the
back for hanging.*

and four candles; a welcome wreath to hang on the door; there are countless ways to adapt the simple basic design.

Florists sell dry foam rings in a range of sizes from 15cm/6in to 30cm/12in which you can cover with dried flowers and preserved leaves, and preformed absorbent foam rings in a plastic base which are suitable for use with evergreens. Then there are all the high-textured twisted twig and clipped grass rings which need the minimum of adornment to make attractive wall decorations.

Here is a chance to turn all your short-stemmed dried flowers, clippings from larger arrangements and even broken stems, to decorative account. Dry foam rings need to be packed tight with plant materials so that not one grain of the silver-sparkly surface is visible; the perfect way to use up all the bits and pieces.

Make your selection for a dried flower circlet with the furnishing scheme well in mind. You may choose pink and blue larkspur – each stem will cut into three or four short lengths for this purpose – cream strawflowers and lacy white sea lavender, a useful ingredient that visually softens the edges of the design. You may choose dried purple sage leaves, tiny dark red rosebuds and clippings of red and green hydrangea heads. Or you may prefer a more rustic look, and decorate a dry foam ring with bunches of wheat ears, small wired pine cones, seedheads and nuts, with sea lavender or dried or preserved leaves to fill in the spaces.

Dried flowers make perfect partners with evergreens for the traditional Christmas decorations, an Advent ring for the table and a welcome wreath for the door. You can use a soaked absorbent foam ring for these designs, covering them completely with short sprays of foliage and adding a galaxy of dried flowers for embellishment.

INDOOR TREES

Indoor trees, sometimes called designer trees, make an unusually pretty use of dried flowers. With all the style of clipped topiary and all the charm of a dried flower arrangement, such trees can be made as table or floor-standing decorations; it depends on the size of the foam sphere you use.

The trees are made of a foam ball pierced on the end of a 'tree trunk' which can be a gnarled twig, a smooth branch, a dried hogweed stem, a dowel wrapped with raffia or a bamboo cane. The dry foam balls which form the heart of the trees are made in sizes from 7.5cm/3in to 25cm/10in in diameter. Allow for the extra width of the dried flower stems pushed into the foam and you can calculate the scale of the finished design.

The tree supports can be planted in ceramic or earthenware pots, in wooden troughs, metal bowls or other suitable containers. You can use well-compacted soil to anchor the support, but florists' setting clay (for small designs) or plaster of Paris give firmer results. If a breakable container is used with clay or plaster of Paris, it should first be lined with slivers cut from a block of dry foam, to allow for expansion of the material and to avoid breakage. Cover the top of the container with a layer of granite chippings, pot-pourri or peat to hide the holding material.

The exciting thing about designer trees is that they can be more floriforous than any known species, can combine flowers of two or more seasons, and can be in any colour range you choose. You might plan a gleaming tree composed of short sprays of silver honesty and orange Chinese lanterns. You might use preserved leaves and multi-coloured strawflowers, or an assortment of varnished nuts for a luxurious effect.

The dry foam spheres have another quite different function, providing the base for hanging-ball designs of all kinds. You can create a romantic design of rosebuds and sea lavender to hang in a bedroom; or see page 79 for another idea.

The instructions and ideas in this book provide all the information – and, we hope, the inspiration – you need to create stunning and individual dried-flower decorations of your own. Enjoy your creations.

ADVENT RING

YOU WILL NEED:

FOAM RING IN PLASTIC BASE
4 PLASTIC CANDLE SPIKES
4 CANDLES
SILVER SPRAY PAINT
TARTAN RIBBON
1 MEDIUM-GAUGE STUB WIRE
—
PRESERVED EVERGREEN LEAVES
SILVER CURRY PLANT LEAVES
WHITE SEA LAVENDER
POPPY SEEDHEADS
RED MINIATURE ROSES

1 *A pre-formed ring in a rigid plastic base makes a perfect holder for your Christmas table decoration. The candles are held in plastic spikes pressed into the foam.*

2 *Sprays of preserved evergreen leaves are arranged at intervals around the ring, some stems angled almost horizontally.*

3 *Sprays of silver curry plant and white sea lavender contrast well with the evergreens. They also lighten the design, and bring a hint of seasonal frost.*

4 *Poppy seedheads — sprayed with silver paint, if you wish — and short sprays of miniature roses nestle among the leaves.*

5 *For a final festive touch, add a tartan bow held in place with a stub wire pressed into the foam.*

GOLDEN TREE

YOU·WILL·NEED:
EARTHENWARE FLOWER POT
STURDY TWIG
BLOCK OF HARD-SETTING CLAY
DRY FOAM SPHERE
GREEN SATIN RIBBON
—
WHITE STATICE
YELLOW STATICE
YELLOW BROOM BLOOM
SPHAGNUM MOSS

1 *The block of clay is pressed into the base of the pot and the twig pushed into it. The foam sphere, pushed on to the top of the twig, is partly covered with short sprays of white statice.*

2 *Statice, which is widely available and relatively cheap, is a good choice for the tree. Yellow sprays are inserted among the white flowers until the foam is almost completely covered.*

3 *Different texture, similar colour – short lengths of yellow broom bloom are added to the design, the stems slightly longer than those of the statice.*

4 *Moss is used to fill the pot and cover the holding material, and a bright ribbon bow is tied just below the flower tree.*

YOU WILL NEED:

DRY FOAM SPHERE

STUB WIRE

STRING

TARTAN RIBBON

—

GREEN WHEAT

GREEN OATS

CREAM STRAWFLOWERS

BLUE-DYED RHODANTHE

RED STRAWFLOWERS

HARE'S-TAIL GRASS

1 *A bent stub wire is pressed into the top of the sphere so that it can be hung on a piece of string. Short, even stems of green wheat are positioned all around the sphere.*

2 *Green oats, cut to the same length as the wheat, continue to build up the design. In place of the cereals you could use decorative grasses or, for a country garden effect, short stems of lavender.*

3 *Cream strawflowers and blue-dyed rhodanthe, the stems cut short and the heads pressed close against the foam, give substance to the design and help to conceal the sphere.*

4 *Red strawflowers and the natural, neutral tone of the fluffy hare's-tail grass complete the design — a striking composition of two primary colours. A tartan ribbon is stapled to the string and finished with a flat bow.*

Index

80